HOLMAN *QuickSource* GUIDE

ATLAS OF
BIBLE LANDS

INTRODUCTION AND TEXT BY
PAUL H. WRIGHT

CONTENTS

INTRODUCTION

"Long ago God spoke to the fathers by the prophets at different times and in different ways. In these last days, He has spoken to us by His Son" (Heb. 1:1-2). The writer of the book of Hebrews reminds us how God revealed Himself to people in the past.

As creator of the universe, God stands outside of time and space. He nevertheless chose to enter a real flesh and blood world in order to create, and then redeem, mankind. For hundreds of years God communicated His words and will to an eager—yet usually recalcitrant —people who made their homes in the lands hugging the southeastern shore of the Mediterranean Sea. Then, in what the Apostle Paul called "the completion of time"(Gal. 4:4), God Himself bent down to enter the human race, choosing to dirty His hands and feet in a small, noisy, and very needy corner of the Roman Empire called Galilee (cp. Phil. 2:5-8).

Unlike sacred books of the world's other great religions, the Bible is full of stories of real people living in real places. God's decision to communicate eternal truths through fallible human beings, to wrap His message around mankind's experiences with rock and soil and water, is both mind-boggling and humbling. It also suggests that a full understanding of God's revelation cannot be gained without an appreciation of the physical context in which that revelation was given.

1 ▶ THE ANCIENT NEAR EAST

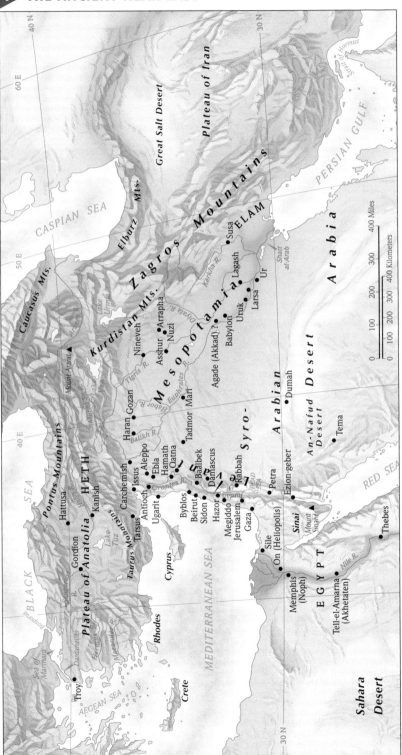

The rugged terrain characteristic of the Wilderness of Judah.

The writers of the Bible knew well the land in which God chose to reveal Himself, for it was their home. They were intimately familiar with the rugged terrain of Judah, with cold winter rain and scorching desert heat, and they had experienced the relief offered by a small spring of water or the shelter of a crevasse in a mighty rock. They knew what it meant for the hills surrounding their city or village to be filled with enemy troops or to lie down at night secure after a bountiful harvest. Time and again the Bible's historians, prophets and poets used such information to enliven the divine message they had to tell. Geographical information fills the biblical text—and the biblical authors assumed that their readers knew even more. The land of the Bible has rightly been termed the "playing board of biblical history" (James M. Monson, *Regions on the Run*, Rockford, IL: Biblical Backgrounds, 1998, p. 3). It is difficult at best to fully understand the instructions (the Bible) without the board (the land) on which the events of the Bible were played out.

Many people journey to the lands of the Bible with the hope of walking where Jesus walked. In spite of the established pilgrimage spots in the Holy Land, however, it is just not possible to say with certainty that Jesus stood on spot "X" when he healed such-and-such a person or delivered such-and-such a teaching. On the other hand, the location of many biblical cities, hills, valleys, and the like are known, and by carefully studying the geographical settings of the Bible, the serious

A calm Sea of Galilee at dusk with snow-capped Mount Hermon in the distance.

reader can enter more deeply into its world. It becomes possible to follow Joshua's army into the hill country of Canaan after laying waste to Jericho. One can climb to the crest of the hill on which David's Jerusalem stood and still experience the energy of the Songs of Ascent (Pss. 121–134). Jesus must have often gazed over the Sea of Galilee in the early mornings from the hills above Capernaum (cp. Mark 1:35); doing so today helps the serious Bible reader appreciate Jesus' call to ministry—and one's own place in the kingdom of God.

There is yet another reason why understanding the geography of Bible lands is important for understanding the Bible. God created the features of the lands of the Bible in the way that He did—and then chose to bring His people there (Gen. 12:1-3; 13:14-17; 15:12-18)— for a reason. In fact, the lands of the Bible are uniquely suited to teach lessons about the nature and character of God as well as the ways that His people should respond to Him.

The various natural features of the lands of the Bible combine to form a setting in which personal or national security was always in doubt. With limited rainfall, an overabundance of rocks but scarcity of good soil, and a position situated alongside a major international highway on which the armies of the world marched, the lands of the Bible were well acquainted with lifestyles that demanded that their inhabitants depend on God to survive. In today's maddening times, the lands of the Bible offer lessons of peace and security that should be heard—and heeded.

The Holman QuickSource Guide: Atlas of Bible Lands has two divisions.

PALESTINE

The first division focuses on the narrow strip of land that is broadly called Palestine, Israel, or the Holy Land. This is the land God promised to Abraham and which came fully under Israel's control during the time of David. This part of the *Atlas* looks at the major regions of Palestine giving attention to the geographical and climatological features of each region.

MAPS OF BIBLE LANDS

The second division of the *QuickSource Atlas* begins with Noah and follows the Bible's story line from Genesis to Revelation showing the places where these events took place.

PALESTINE

Most of the events described in the Bible took place within the borders of the modern state of Israel plus the West Bank and areas currently under the Palestinian Authority. For many Bible readers this entire region should be called *Israel*, while others prefer the term *Palestine*. Theological or political considerations usually play a decisive role in what this land is called today, just as they have throughout history. Indeed, theological and political positions often claim support from names found on a map. The names Canaan, Israel, and Palestine (or Palestina) have all been used at various times in history to designate the land that lies between the Mediterranean Sea and the Jordan River. When speaking geographically, however, Bible atlases and encyclopedias commonly refer to this land as Palestine rather than Israel, without intending to make a religious or political statement. For this reason, the term *Palestine* is used in this volume as well.

2 ▶ MODERN POLITICAL DIVISIONS OF ANCIENT PALESTINE

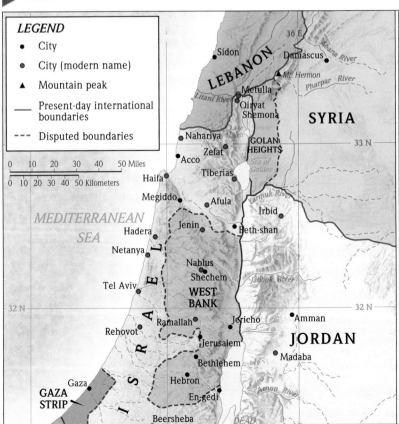

LEGEND
- City
- City (modern name)
- ▲ Mountain peak
- ___ Present-day international boundaries
- --- Disputed boundaries

0 10 20 30 40 50 Miles
0 10 20 30 40 50 Kilometers

Sidon · Damascus · Abana River
LEBANON · Mt. Hermon · Pharpar River
Litani River · Metulla · Qiryat Shemona · SYRIA
Nahariya · Lake Hula · GOLAN HEIGHTS · 33 N
Zefat · Sea of Galilee
Acco · Tiberias
Haifa
Megiddo · Afula · Yarmuk River
MEDITERRANEAN SEA · Jenin · Irbid · Beth-shan
Hadera
Netanya
Nablus · Jabbok River
Shechem
Tel Aviv · WEST BANK
32 N · Ramallah · Jericho · Amman · 32 N
Rehovot · Jerusalem · JORDAN
Bethlehem · Madaba
Gaza · Hebron
GAZA STRIP · En-gedi · Arnon River
Beersheba · DEAD
ISRAEL

Some biblical events took place in lands that lie outside of the modern state of Israel. These lands include Egypt, Mesopotamia (modern Iraq), Persia (modern Iran), Edom Moab and Ammon (all in modern Jordan), Phoenicia (modern Lebanon), Aram (modern Syria), regions such as Galatia, Phrygia, Lydia and Mysia (all in modern Turkey), Macedonia and Achaia (both in modern Greece), Cyprus, Crete, and Italy. Other lands in North Africa (Libya and Cyrene), or located in the Arabian peninsula or in northeastern Africa (Cush and Sheba), are also mentioned in the Bible. Each of these is properly a "land of the Bible," as well, and should be of interest to serious Bible readers.

3 ▶ MODERN STATES AND THE ANCIENT NEAR EAST

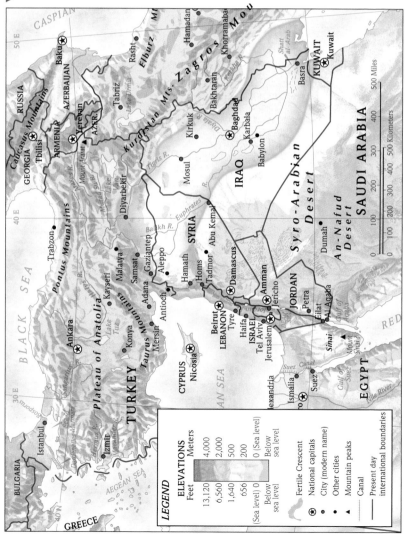

Names for the Bible Lands

CANAAN

The origin of the word *Canaan* remains uncertain. Some relate it to the Akkadian word for a costly blue-purple dye (*kinahhu*)—or the cloth dyed that color—that was derived from murex shells found along the Phoenician coast. Others find its origins in the Akkadian word designating a class or type of merchants (*kina 'nu*) dealing in this type of dyed cloth. Support for this latter suggestion is found in passages such as Isaiah 23:8 and Zephaniah 1:11.

ISRAEL

Genesis 32:28 connects the name *Israel* with a Hebrew verb meaning "to struggle or strive": "Your name will no longer be Jacob, but Israel, because you have struggled with God and with men and have overcome" (NIV). It is unclear, however, whether the author of Genesis 32 is providing the actual etymology of the word or simply punning on the name *Israel*.

PALESTINE

Palestine is derived from the word *Philistine*. It was first used by the Greek historian Herodotus in the fifth century B.C. to refer to the geographical area of the southeastern Mediterranean coast. Some English editions of the KJV uses *Palestina* as an alternate name for Philistia in Exodus 15:14 and Isaiah 14:29,31.

HOLY LAND

The term *holy land*, so familiar to Christians as a synonym of Israel, is in fact a very rare biblical term. Its only true occurrence is Zechariah 2:12, part of a vivid prophecy of the restoration of Israel: "The LORD will inherit Judah as his portion in the holy land, and will again choose Jerusalem." The HCSB, NIV, NASB, and RSV also mention the "holy land" in Psalm 78:54: "Thus he brought them (i.e., Israel) to the border of his holy land, to the hill country his right hand had taken." The NKJV, reading the Hebrew text more literally, however, translates this phrase as "His holy border" instead.

▲ At just over 8,000 square miles, Palestine is about the size of New Jersey, but its variations in topography and climate more closely resemble those of California.

Climate

The climate of Palestine is largely a product of the land's narrow dimensions between desert and sea. The vast Arabian Desert to the east of the rift valley encroaches to within less than 100 miles of the Mediterranean, pinching Palestine between an extremely hot, dry desert climate and the more temperate climate of the sea. Moreover, in the Sinai Peninsula to the south, the eastern extremity of the Sahara meets the Arabian Desert, and both touch the Mediterranean coast. Because Palestine is narrowly wedged between the desert and the sea, any minor change in global weather patterns will have significant or even drastic effects on its annual climate.

Palestine's climate is also affected by topography. Because of sharp variations in topography, the local climate within Palestine can differ widely in a space of just a few miles. The main ridge forming the backbone of the hill country—the watershed ridge—runs north-northeast to south-southwest, at right angles to the prevailing rains off the Mediterranean. Most of the rain that falls in Palestine falls on the western side of the watershed ridge, leaving the eastern slopes and the rift valley under a dry rain shadow. Rain also falls in a narrow north-south band in the higher hills that rise east of the rift but quickly tapers off further east under the harsh effects of the Arabian Desert.

That is, higher elevations in the northwestern part of the country receive ample amounts of rainfall, while lower elevations to the southeast receive scant rainfall. Mount Carmel, which juts into the Mediterranean Sea in the northern part of the country, receives over 32 inches of rainfall per year. By contrast, the Dead Sea, only 80 miles to the southeast but below sea level, receives less than two inches of rainfall per year. Jerusalem receives about 25 inches of rain per year, about the same as London, but unlike London, all the rain of Jerusalem falls over the course of five or six months.

4 ▶ CROSS SECTIONAL VIEWS OF LONGITUDINAL ZONES

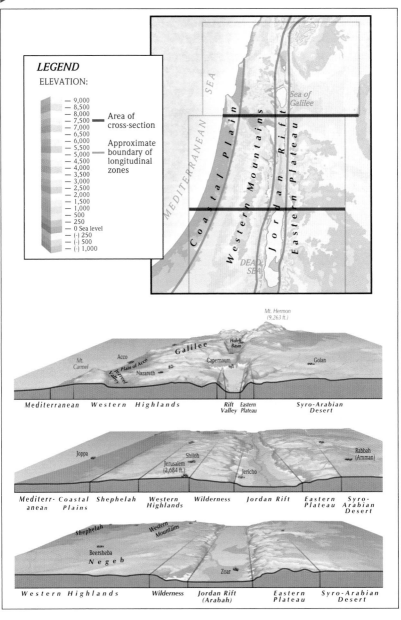

LEGEND

ELEVATION:

- 9,000
- 8,500
- 8,000
- 7,500 — Area of cross-section
- 7,000
- 6,500
- 6,000
- 5,500 — Approximate boundary of longitudinal zones
- 5,000
- 4,500
- 4,000
- 3,500
- 3,000
- 2,500
- 2,000
- 1,500
- 1,000
- 500
- 250
- 0 Sea level
- (-) 250
- (-) 500
- (-) 1,000

It is possible to speak in general of three "rules of rainfall" for Palestine:
1) north is wet, south is dry
2) west is wet, east is dry
3) high is wet; low is dry

There are two primary seasons in Palestine, a rainy season (usually mid-October through mid-April) and a dry season (usually mid-May through September). Short transitional seasons mark the change between the two. Palestine's agricultural year is determined by these seasons, as were the times of ancient Israel's major festivals (see below).

▼ THE AGRICULTURAL YEAR

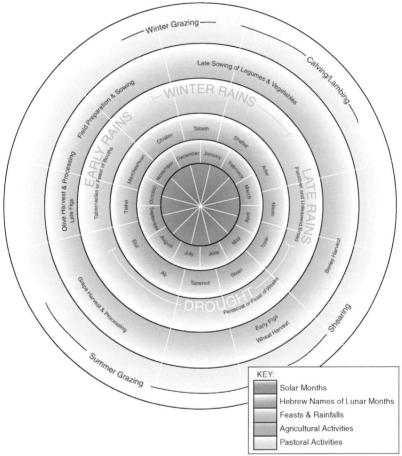

KEY:
- Solar Months
- Hebrew Names of Lunar Months
- Feasts & Rainfalls
- Agricultural Activities
- Pastoral Activities

The rainy season begins with the early rains of late October and November. These rains clear the air of dust and loosen the soil for planting grain (Deut. 11:14; Ps. 84:5-7; Jer. 5:24; Joel 2:23; cp. Ps. 65:10). If the rains are late, farmers anticipate famine (cp. Prov. 25:14; Amos 4:7). The early rains are followed by heavy winter rains that fall in December, January, and February (Ezra 10:9-13). During the winter months, storms typically roll into Palestine from the northwest, dumping heavy waves of rain for three or four days. Between storms, the land experiences clear, sunny skies and moderate temperatures. The storms lessen in March and early April, as the latter rains give the heads of grain their final growth (cp. Zech. 10:1; Mark 4:28).

Snow falls every year on Mount Hermon, but only some winters in other parts of Palestine. Snow typically falls at night (temperatures rarely dip below freezing during the daytime) and in the higher elevations of the hill country (above 1,700 feet); it is wet and heavy, and usually melts the next day (cp. Job 24:19). Snow was rare enough in ancient Israel to receive special notice by the biblical writers (e.g., 1 Chron. 11:22; Job 6:15-16; 38:22-23).

5 ▶ CLIMATE PATTERNS OF ANCIENT PALESTINE

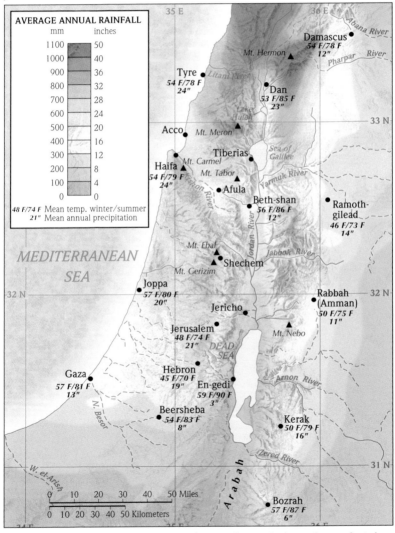

The average August daytime temperature in Jerusalem, a city located 2,600 feet above sea level, is 86° Fahrenheit; at night, the temperature averages 64°. The highest temperature ever recorded in Palestine was 129° Fahrenheit on June 21, 1945, near Beth Shan in the upper Jordan Valley. On May 24, 1999, Jericho set a record temperature of 124° Fahrenheit. Both Beth Shan and Jericho lie below sea level in the rift valley.

Natural Routes

What Palestine lacks in natural resources, it makes up for in location. Palestine's geopolitical importance lies in its role as a passageway between three great land masses, Africa, Europe, and Asia, as well as between the Mediterranean Sea and the Red Sea (Indian Ocean). Because the land is bisected by major trade routes, political powers who controlled Palestine during the biblical period become major economic players in the ancient Near East, just as they do in the modern Middle East today. Routes that carry trade, however, also carry armies, and throughout history Palestine has been overrun numerous times as foreign powers have sought to secure the region for themselves. The international routes that cross Palestine also make the land a meeting place of cultures where new ways of life and faith challenge those that have already taken root in its soil.

6 INTERNATIONAL ROUTES

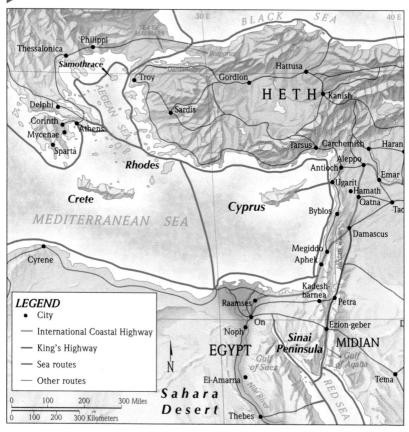

"There is no land which is at once so much a sanctuary and an observatory as Palestine; no land which, till its office was fulfilled, was so swept by the great forces of history, and was yet so capable of preserving one tribe in national continuity and growth; one tribe learning and suffering and rising superior to the successive problems these forces presented to her, till upon the opportunity afforded by the last of them she launched her results upon the world" (George Adam Smith, *The Historical Geography of the Holy Land*, Hodder & Stoughton, 1931, p. 91).

It is possible to reconstruct many of the important routes of ancient Palestine by comparing the location of the land's gravitation points (e.g., population centers, gateway cities, seaports, and the like) with topographical features that act either as channels for traffic or barriers to travel. For instance, in the rugged Cenomanian hill country, most traffic stayed on the tops of ridges, with the primary routes into and out of the hills following the continuous ridges that separate wadi systems (e.g., "the road going up to Beth Horon," Josh. 10:10 NIV). Routes tended to follow the easiest—but not necessarily the shortest—distance between two points, avoiding where possible rugged mountainous regions, swampy and sandy areas, and deserts. Most of the natural routes of antiquity can still be followed, even though, thanks to modern road building machinery, many highways in Israel today violate the land's natural topography.

It is also possible to reconstruct ancient routes in Palestine by looking at the movement of persons through the land in the biblical story. For instance, we read that Abraham entered Canaan from the north, stopped at Shechem and Bethel, then continued south toward the Negev (Gen. 12:4-9). [See **THE MIGRATION OF ABRAHAM**, p. 74] In doing so he followed a well-worn natural route through the middle of the hill country, a route that in part makes use of the watershed ridge forming the spine of the hill country of Judah. The portion of this "Patriarchal Highway" that goes through the hill country of Ephraim was described in detail by the writer of Judges (Judg. 21:19).

Many local routes crisscrossed Palestine. The Bible provides the names of some of these. Typically a road was named after its destination (e.g., "the road to Shur"—Gen. 16:7; "the road toward Bashan"—Num. 21:33; "the way to the wasteland of Gibeon"—2 Sam. 2:24, etc. [NIV]). "The king's highway" (Num. 20:17) is the only clear biblical exception to this rule (but cp. Isa. 35:8). [Several important routes are shown on **INTERNATIONAL ROUTES**, p.16]

Two major international routes ran the length of Palestine in antiquity, one west of the rift valley and the other to the east (p.16). The western route is often called the International Coastal Highway or *Via Maris* ("the Way of the Sea"). The biblical name "the road through the Philistine country" (Exod. 13:17 NIV) refers to the southern portion of this route as it hugs the Mediterranean coast in the vicinity of Gaza. Historically, the International Coastal Highway was the principal highway carrying international traffic between Egypt and Mesopotamia. North of Damascus, this route followed the arc of the Fertile Crescent, but once in Palestine it worked its way through the hills and valleys of Galilee to the coast. Strategic cities in Palestine along this route in the biblical period (from north to south) were Hazor, Megiddo, Aphek, Gezer, and Gaza.

The eastern international route ran due south out of Damascus through the highlands of northern Transjordan to Rabbath-ammon (modern Amman, Jordan). From here one branch connected the capital cities of the Old Testament nations of Ammon, Moab, and Edom (Rabbath-ammon, Kir-hareseth, and Bozrah, respectively) before continuing south to the Red Sea and the great inland spice route of Arabia. The Bible calls this route "the king's highway" (Num. 20:17; 21:22 NIV). An eastern branch, the "desert road of Moab" (Deut. 2:8), skirted Moab and Edom along the edge of the desert. Less a route of armies, the international highway in Transjordan carried the wealth of the Arabian Peninsula (e.g., gold, frankincense, and myrrh) to the empires of the ancient Near Eastern and Mediterranean worlds.

Roman Roads

In the late first and early second centuries A.D., the Romans built an extensive road system in Palestine, part of a larger road system tying together their far-flung empire. For the most part these roads followed the old natural routes of the biblical period but with sophisticated technological improvements (e.g., grading, curbing, paving, etc). Some of the mileposts marking these roads remain allowing intrepid hikers to follow their course today. Jesus often walked between Jericho and Jerusalem (Matt. 20:29; cp. Luke 10:30); in His travels He no doubt followed the natural route which was upgraded to the status of a Roman road about a hundred years later.

Eventually larger powers—the Assyrians (2 Kings 15:29), Babylonians, Persians, Greeks, Seleucids, Ptolemies, and Romans—seized the Huleh Basin to secure their position in the area. By New Testament times, the Huleh sat in the middle of Jewish and Gentile populations. In offering the wealth and opportunities of the world, this region became a true testing ground of faith.

THE LAND OF PALESTINE

The land of Palestine can be divided a number of ways. For the purpose of the *QuickSource Atlas*, we will look at four broad regions: the southern regions (Judah/Judea), the central regions (Israel/Samaria), the northern regions (Galilee), and the eastern regions (Transjordan).

A view from the front of the treasury building of the narrow entryway into the Nabatean city of Petra.

THE SOUTHERN REGIONS
(Judah/Judaea)

The southern portion of Palestine, generally corresponding to the land of the Southern Kingdom of Judah, is composed of six distinct geographical regions: the hill country of Judah, the Shephelah, the Philistine coastal plain, the biblical Negev, the wilderness of Judah and the land of Benjamin.

7 ▶ PHILISTINE PLAIN, SHEPHELAH, JUDAH, AND THE DEAD SEA

The Hill Country of Judah

The hill country of Judah formed the heartland of the Old Testament kingdom of Judah, as well as the New Testament province, Judea. In area the hill country covers approximately 480 square miles (40 miles x 12 miles), the size of an average county in the United States. The high point of the hill country, at Halhul (cp. Josh. 15:58) just north of Hebron, is 3,347 feet in elevation.

> *Joshua 10:40, summarizing Joshua's conquests in the southern part of Canaan, recognizes the natural geographical regions of the land of Judah: "So Joshua subdued the whole region, including the hill country, the Negev, the western foothills and the mountain slopes, together with all their kings." In this translation (NIV), "western foothills" translates the Hebrew term* shephelah, *while "mountain slopes" refers to the wilderness slopes to the east. Similar verses are Deuteronomy 1:7 and Jeremiah 17:26.*

8 ▶ JOSHUA'S CENTRAL AND SOUTHERN CAMPAIGNS

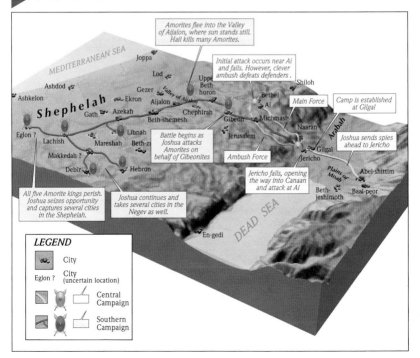

Amorites flee into the Valley of Aijalon, where sun stands still. Hail kills many Amorites.

Initial attack occurs near Ai and fails. However, clever ambush defeats defenders.

Camp is established at Gilgal

Main Force

Joshua sends spies ahead to Jericho

Battle begins as Joshua attacks Amorites on behalf of Gibeonites

Ambush Force

Jericho falls, opening the way into Canaan and attack at Ai

All five Amorite kings perish. Joshua seizes opportunity and captures several cities in the Shephelah.

Joshua continues and takes several cities in the Negev as well.

MEDITERRANEAN SEA
Joppa
Lod
Ashdod
Ashkelon
Gezer
Ekron
Aijalon
Shephelah
Gath
Azekah
Beth-shemesh
Chephirah
Upper Beth-horon
Valley of Aijalon
Bethel
Ai
Gibeon
Michmash
Shiloh
Naaran
Arabah
Gilgal
Jericho
Plains of Moab
Abel-shittim
Beth-jeshimoth
Baal-peor
Jerusalem
Libnah
Mareshah
Beth-zur
Lachish
Eglon ?
Makkedah ?
Debir
Hebron
En-gedi
DEAD SEA

LEGEND

City	
Eglon ?	City (uncertain location)
	Central Campaign
	Southern Campaign

The wadi through the limestone cliffs of the Qumran area in Israel.

The watershed ridge, running north-northeast by south-southwest, forms the backbone of the hill country of Judah. From it, wadis flow westward to the Mediterranean Sea and eastward to the Jordan Valley and Dead Sea. As these wadis cut through the hard Cenomanian limestone, they form deep, V-shaped valleys with steep, rugged sides. Because the limestone is bedded, it breaks on the wadi slopes into natural terraces that have been improved with considerable effort through the centuries into numerous small but fertile plots of agricultural land. Adequate winter rainfall, plentiful springs, and rich terra rosa soil have allowed farmers and villagers in the hill country of Judah to produce ample crops to sustain life. Since antiquity the traditional crops of the hill country have been grapes, figs, olives, pomegranates and almonds (cp. Deut. 8:8). Grapes, figs, and olives, in addition to bread, were the staples of life.

Pomegranate blossoms taken at Sabaste, Israel.

Young grapes growing near Tel Lakhish (Isa. 5:1-7).

From earliest times, the traditional crops of the Judean hill country have had symbolic value. Grapes symbolized a full life of serenity and peace (1 Kings 4:24; Ps. 128:3) and, in particular, people living under the blessing of God (Ps. 80:8-11,14-15; John 15:1-7). Figs, identified with the tree of knowledge (cp. Gen. 3:7), were also a symbol of prosperity and peace (Isa. 36:16; Hab. 3:17). Biblical writers used olive trees to speak of beauty, fertility, and endurance (Gen. 8:11; Ps. 128:3). Pomegranates symbolized beauty, love, and fertility (Song 4:3,13), and the almond, blooming in mid-January as the harbinger of spring, hearkened to the hastening of events (Num. 17:8; Eccles. 12:5; Jer. 1:11-12).

The major cities of the hill country of Judah—Hebron, Bethlehem, and Jerusalem—are located just off the central watershed ridge. They are linked together by the main route through the hill country, the central ridge route or Patriarchal Highway, which follows the line of this ridge. Of the hill country cities, Hebron has always held pride of place in terms of geographical and agricultural advantage, and it was there that David, born in Bethlehem and destined to find glory in Jerusalem, first reigned as king over Israel (2 Sam. 5:1-5).

Countryside between Jerusalem and Bethlehem.
Olive trees can be seen in a small orchard.

The rugged wadis that drop out of the hill country tend to isolate the cities and villages of the watershed ridge from the International Coastal Highway to the west and the rift valley and King's Highway to the east (see **INTERNATIONAL ROUTES**, p.16). A few natural routes following the continuous ridges that divide these wadi systems link Hebron, Bethlehem, and Jerusalem to the world beyond. Down one of these ridges that connects Bethlehem with the Elah Valley in the Shephelah (the "Husan Ridge Route"), a young David brought food to his brothers fighting the Philistines (1 Sam. 17:12-19). It was probably along this same route that Philip met an Ethiopian eunuch traveling from Jerusalem to Gaza (Acts 8:26-40).

Because of its rugged isolation and natural defenses, Judah has always been relatively closed to foreign cultural influences. The large powers of antiquity (Egypt, Assyria, Babylon, Greece, and Rome) were occasionally drawn into the hill country to fight against the Canaanites, Israelites, or Jews living in Jerusalem but seldom went out of their way to settle there. As a result, the local inhabitants of Judah tended to value stable and conservative lifestyles. It was here that Jeremiah preached the "old time religion" of Moses, that Isaiah spoke of a coming messiah to deliver His people (Isa. 40:9-11) and that Judaism took its formative steps in the centuries leading up to the New Testament. More than any other region in Palestine, the hill country of Judah represents the land in which God chose to dwell among His people.

During the biblical period, the hill country of Judah was the "irreducible minimum" of God's promised land, the cradle of Israelite and Jewish life. On its protected ridges and slopes God's people were given opportunity to take root and prosper. Their success was mixed and depended on their willingness to obey Him (Deut. 11:11-12; 28:1-68; Ps. 80:1-19).

The Shephelah

The Shephelah (lit. "lowland," translated "western foothills" by the NIV) is the area of low, rolling Eocene hills between the hill country of Judah and the coastal plain (Deut. 1:7; Josh. 9:1; 10:40; 15:33-36; 1 Kings 10:27; 2 Chron. 26:10; Jer. 17:26). This region covers approximately 250 square miles (25 miles x 10 miles), and its hills vary in elevation from 300 to 1,200 feet.

A hard mineral crust called nari, three to five feet thick, covers the hills of the Shephelah, rendering them practically useless for agriculture. Only small trees and shrubs grow on these hills naturally. The broad valleys of the Shephelah, however, are quite fertile and particularly well suited for grain (wheat and barley), but vineyards and orchard crops also do well there. These valleys are the extension of the major wadi systems flowing west out of the hill country of Judah and are fed by ample run-off rainfall from the hills.

Five Valleys of the Shephelah have figured prominently in the political history of Palestine. From north to south, they are the Aijalon, the Sorek, the Elah, the Guvrin, and the Lachish.

Several verses in the Bible mention the agricultural possibilities of the Shephelah. 1 Chronicles 27:28 mentions the sycamore tree, which produces an inferior type of fig, and the olive tree.

The Lachish Valley is named after Lachish, the second most important city in Judah during the late monarchy. The capture of Lachish by the Assyrian king Sennacherib in 701 B.C. (2 Kings 18:14,17; 19:8) and again by the Babylonian king Nebuchadnezzar in 587 B.C. (Jer. 34:7) signaled the fall of the entire Shephelah to foreign powers.

The definitive line of a wall at Lachish running from the south, northeast up to the high place.

Politically, the Shephelah has always functioned as both a bridge and a buffer between the hill country and the coastal plain. The east-west orientation of the five valleys of the Shephelah provides easy access for the people of the coast to move into the hill country (e.g., the Philistines or international powers such as Egypt, Assyria, Babylon, Greece, and Rome). On the other hand, if the inhabitants of the hill country are to have any thoughts of expanding their influence in Palestine, they must first secure the agricultural lands and highways of the Shephelah. For this reason, the valleys of the Shephelah historically have functioned like saloon doors of the Old West, swinging either in or out depending on the strength and ability of those pushing from either side. At times, however, a king in Jerusalem would attempt to close the doors altogether, building fortifications in the Shephelah as a front guard for his heartland in the hill country (2 Chron. 11:5-12).

As Judah's buffer zone toward the coast, the Shephelah witnessed assault after assault on Jerusalem. This was the region that Judah could scarcely afford to lose yet over time could scarcely control.

The Philistine Coastal Plain

 The western summit of Mount Carmel overlooking the modern Israeli port city of Haifa.

Palestine's coastal plain stretches from north of Mount Carmel to the Sinai Peninsula. The portion of this plain that lies between the Yarqon River, a stream flowing through Joppa (the modern city of Tel Aviv), and the Nahal Besor just south of Gaza is commonly known as the Philistine coastal plain. This was the heartland of the Philistines during much of the time of the Old Testament.

The Philistine coastal plain extends approximately 50 miles along the Mediterranean coast, varying in width from 10 miles in the north to 25 miles in the south. The plain rises gradually eastward to the hills of the Shephelah. Sand dunes dominate the coastline, but inland the sand mixes with alluvial and loess soils (from the Shephelah and Negev, respectively) to form a decent agricultural base. Historically, the major agricultural crops grown on the coastal plain have been grain, but citrus orchards are common in the area today.

9 MEDITERRANEAN COASTLINE

LEGEND
- City
- International Coastal Highway
- King's Highway
- Sea routes
- Other routes

MEDITERRANEAN SEA

Sidon · Damascus · Tyre · Dan · Hazor · Capernaum · Acco · Yokneam · Megiddo · Jezreel · Ramoth-gilead · Beth-shan · Socoh · Shechem · Joppa · Aphek · Amman · Ashdod · Ekron · Jerusalem · Heshbon · Medeba · Gaza · Dibon · Beersheba · Kir-hareseth · Bozrah · Punon

N

The shoreline of the Mediterranean coast is stiff and uninviting except for a small natural harbor at Joppa (modern Tel Aviv), Judah's desired seaport. For this reason, most traffic on the plain during the biblical period was land-based, moving north and south along two branches of the International Coastal Highway. One branch, tracking just behind the coastal dunes, linked Gaza, Ashkelon, Ashdod, and Joppa before turning inland to Aphek (1 Sam. 4:1; New Testament Antipatris, Acts 23:31), located at the head of the Yarqon River. An inland branch followed the western edge of the Shephelah, connecting Gerar, Gath, and Ekron to Aphek.

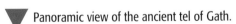

▼ Panoramic view of the ancient tel of Gath.

The openness of the Philistine coastal plain makes this a true international region. This was the homeland of the Philistines, and from their five cities (Gaza, Ashkelon, Ashdod, Ekron, and Gath, 1 Sam. 6:17-18) the Philistines attempted to push into the hill country at the same time that Israel was trying to expand its influence toward the coast.

Eventually large powers from the outside—Assyria and Babylon from the east, Greece and Rome from the west—swept down the coastal plain with their eye on the wealth of Egypt, running over the local inhabitants in the process. The Philistines disappeared from history, although their name lives on in the term "Palestine." The Israelites and Judeans, able to find refuge in the rugged hill country to the east, survived as the spiritual ancestors of both Jews and Christians today.

The Philistine coastal plain was the highway of southern Palestine. Judah wanted to take advantage of the opportunities that living on this highway offered but, more often than not, was run over by mighty empires of the day in the process.

The Biblical Negev

 Excavated storerooms at the site of ancient Beer-sheba in the Negev.

The biblical Negev (lit. "dry land" or "south") is a geological depression reaching inland from the southern Philistine coastal plain to a point 12 miles west of the southern end of the Dead Sea. The western basin of the Negev overlaps the southern end of the coastal plain, and the city of Gerar rightly belongs to both regions. The Negev was the natural southern border of the United Kingdom of Israel (1 Kings 4:25) and the Southern Kingdom of Judah (2 Kings 23:8).

Topographically, the biblical Negev is composed of three broad, shallow basins joined end to end and oriented west to east. These Negev basins receive, on average, 8 to 12 inches of rain per year. When plowed, their powdery, windblown loess soil can retain sufficient water to grow grain. More often than not, however, the rainfall is inadequate for agriculture, and so historically the Negev has been more a land of the shepherd than a land of the farmer. As with the coastal plain, the water table under the Negev basins is high, allowing the residents to dig wells without much difficulty (Gen. 21:25-34; 26:17-33). The arid Negev was a suitable home for the bedouin lifestyle of Abraham, Isaac and Jacob (Gen.13:1-7; 25: 27; 26:12-17).

Ancient Israel was never at home in this "vast and dreadful desert." Solomon was able to pierce the wilderness all the way to Ezion-geber (near modern Eilat), where he sailed his ships on the Red Sea (1 Kings 9:26), but 80 years later Jehoshaphat failed in an attempt to do the same (1 Kings 22:48-49; 2 Chron. 20:35-37). Archaeological excavations have found numerous small settlements throughout the Negev Highlands, perhaps evidence of attempts by strong Judean kings such as Uzziah to settle the region (2 Kings 26:10); they were successful only when Edom could be contained in the southern hills opposite the rift valley (cp. 1 Kings 22:47). By New Testament times this entire region had been taken over by the Nabateans, traders from the eastern mountains, who controlled the traffic in spices from Arabia to Gaza and the Mediterranean Sea.

The biblical Negev was Judah's doorway to the south. For ancient Israel, its value lay not in natural resources but in its strategic position fronting Egypt, Edom, and the great trade routes of the desert.

The Wilderness of Judah

The wilderness of Judea as viewed toward the Dead Sea from atop the Herodium.

Tucked between the hill country of Judah and the rift valley, the wilderness of Judah is the largest area of exposed Senonian chalk west of the Jordan River. In a distance of 10 to 12 miles the ground drops over 4,600 feet from the watershed ridge to the surface of the Dead Sea, which, at more than 1,300 feet below sea level, is the lowest spot on the face of the earth. The view east from the watershed ridge is dramatic and has been likened to a sailor standing on the narrow deck of a huge ship with the angry billows—here a jumbled mass of brown-white chalk hills, rounded and bare—churning below.

The Dead Sea, 50 miles long by 11 miles wide, is the lowest spot on earth (approximately 1,350 feet below sea level), and by far the world's saltiest body of water.

The minerals of the Dead Sea include sodium, magnesium, calcium chloride, bromide, sulfur, potassium, potash and bitumen; these account for 33–38% of the content of the Dead Sea by weight, compared to a 15% mineral content in the Great Salt Lake and 3–3.5% in the oceans. Surprisingly, eleven kinds of bacteria live in the Dead Sea, and some fish congregate around the mouth of the Jordan River. The name "Dead Sea" is really a misnomer, for since antiquity the mineral content in the water has been known to provide healing for a variety of diseases. The Dead Sea's high salt content makes it virtually impossible for a person to sink in its waters.

Two Hebrew terms designate the wilderness of Judah. The more common, *midbar*, refers to the higher areas of the wilderness, where shepherds are able to graze sheep and goats during the winter months (1 Sam. 17:28; Jer. 9:10). The more remote areas, south and east, are called Jeshimon, "waste" or "desert" places, where even the shepherd would not go. It was to the Jeshimon that David retreated when fleeing from Saul (1 Sam. 23:19; 26:1-3).

While many Americans may associate the term "wilderness" with dense woods, the wilderness of Judah is exactly the opposite. The Judean wilderness brings the harsh conditions of the desert to the doorstep of Jerusalem. The biblical writers often used the hard life of the wilderness to illustrate God's judgment and the need for His people to depend on Him.

In the biblical period, the only spots of permanent settlement in the wilderness were at the edge of the rift valley where a few springs provide water (e.g., Jericho, Engedi) and in a small valley above the cliffs west of the northern end of the Dead Sea (the Buqei'a), where runoff rainfall can collect from the hills. Two small towns in the hill country at the edge of the wilderness, Anathoth and Tekoa, were the homes of Jeremiah and Amos respectively. These prophets spoke vividly of the wilderness or wilderness-like conditions in their prophetic messages (e.g., Jer. 2:6; 3:2-3,21; 6:1-5; 9:1-2; 17:5-6; Amos 2:10; 4:7-12). One difficult natural route leads from Bethlehem to Engedi through Tekoa; another drops from Jerusalem to Jericho, skirting Anathoth on the way. The rest of the wilderness is essentially devoid of water supplies and human habitation.

The only natural waterfall in Israel is located at Engedi on the west side of the Dead Sea.

The Land of Benjamin

Joshua allotted the tribe of Benjamin a narrow strip of land wedged between the hill country of Judah to the south and Ephraim to the north (Josh. 18:11-28). Benjamin's territory climbs from the Jordan River up the harsh hills of the wilderness and over the central watershed ridge to the city of Kiriath-jearim, overlooking the western slopes of the hill country. The land of Benjamin is thus a cross section of the hill country of Palestine, with the eastern half the land of the shepherd and the western half the land of the farmer.

Benjamin's allotment included four important cities critical for anyone seeking to control the hill country. The first, the oasis city of Jericho (the City of Palms—Deut. 34:3; Judg. 3:13), is the gateway into central and southern Palestine from the east (Josh. 2:1; 1 Kings 16:34). The second, Bethel, faces the powerful tribes of Ephraim and Manasseh to the north (Gen. 28:19; 1 Kings 12:29; 2 Kings 2:2-3). The third, Gibeon, lying just west of the watershed ridge, is Benjamin's gateway to the Aijalon Valley, Gezer and the west (Josh. 9:1–10:15). The fourth, facing south, is Jerusalem, allotted to Benjamin but conquered by David as his own royal city (2 Sam. 5:6-10). Each of these was an important Canaanite city in the days of Joshua.

Round Neolithic defense tower at Old Testament Jericho.

As the watershed ridge passes through the land of Benjamin, it broadens into a smallish plateau about 25 square miles in size. This "central Benjamin plateau" is actually a broad saddle in the hill country, slightly lower in elevation than the hill country to the north and south. Four cities that play a prominent role in the biblical story lie on the plateau: Gibeah (the hometown of king Saul, 1 Sam. 10:26; 15:34); Ramah (the hometown of Samuel, 1 Sam. 2:11; 8:4; 15:34); Mizpah (the administrative capital of the hill country after the destruction of Jerusalem by the Babylonians, 2 Kings 25:23-25); and Gibeon. Gibeah, Ramah, and Mizpah are located on the Patriarchal Highway, south to north, with Gibeon to the west. Bethel lies on a smaller and higher plateau three miles north of Mizpah, while Jerusalem is the same distance south of Gibeah. The many biblical events that took place in and around these cities testify to the critical importance of the land of Benjamin.

The central Benjamin plateau is well watered, and its terra rosa soil and relatively flat topography combine to form a highly desirable agricultural area. The nahals Aijalon and Sorek drain the plateau to the west and south, while the Wadi Qilt cuts dramatically through the chalk wilderness eastward from the plateau. Several powerful springs in the Wadi Qilt combine to provide a steady flow of water to the plains around Jericho.

View from atop the tel of New Testament Jericho showing the lush greenery of the oasis.

Herod the Great built a large and elaborate summer palace on the banks of the Qilt where the wadi spills out onto the plains of Jericho. His palace contained sumptuous reception and banqueting halls, a Roman bath complex, a sunken garden, a swimming pool, and an arched bridge spanning the wadi. Recent archaeological excavations on the site have also uncovered what is thought to have been a synagogue dating to the first century B.C., the oldest known in Palestine to date. New Testament Jericho grew up around Herod's palace and the adjacent lands of his influential friends. Here Zacchaeus collected taxes for Rome. Jesus' encounter with Zacchaeus showed his followers and critics alike what true repentance really was (Luke 19:1-10).

The central Benjamin plateau is the heartland not only of Benjamin but also of the entire hill country and the scene of much of the biblical story. A look at the sweep of biblical history shows that the people of the land of Benjamin lived in a true testing ground of faith. It is therefore with great significance that the Apostle Paul identified himself as a Benjaminite (Rom. 11:1).

Jerusalem

The biblical writers held Jerusalem in high esteem. Verses such as Psalm 48:1-2 ("His holy mountain, rising splendidly"), Psalm 122:1 ("Let us go to"), and Isaiah 2:2-3 ("it will be raised above the hills," NIV) are rooted in soaring theological expectations about God's chosen city. At the same time, they are also grounded in the physical reality of the land. Jerusalem is a city of hills and valleys, and most steps taken on its streets either go up or down. Today Jerusalem is a beautiful city, with surprising vistas and new horizons as the sun and clouds play upon its huddled mass of gray to golden walls, domes and towers; the same, from all accounts, was also true in antiquity (cp. Song 6:4).

> *The Talmud, Judaism's monumental codification of the oral law, speaks of Jerusalem in lofty terms: "Whoever has not seen Jerusalem in its splendor has never seen a lovely city" (Succah 51b); and "Of the ten measures of beauty that came down to the world, Jerusalem took nine" (Kidushin 49b).*

Historically, the Kidron and Hinnom Valleys have marked the limits of settlement in Jerusalem, although over the course of the last 150 years the city has spilled over the surrounding hills and valleys on every side. The Kidron Valley, on the east, separates the old walled city from the Mount of Olives. The Hinnom Valley (the "Valley of the Sons of Hinnom") curls around the western and southern sides of the city, with the watershed ridge and Patriarchal Highway beyond. The Hinnom formed the border between the tribal inheritances of Judah (to the south and west) and Benjamin (to the north and east) (Josh. 18:16). North of the city the ground rises gradually, without natural defense, and this has been the preferred direction of attack since antiquity.

It was in the southern portion of the "Valley of the Sons of Hinnom" (Hb. *ge bene-hinnom*) that kings Ahaz and Manassah of Judah apparently sacrificed their sons by fire to the pagan god Molech (2 Kings 21:6; 2 Chron. 28:3; cp. 2 Kings 23:10). Some scholars think that the ancient Israelites also dumped refuse from the city into the Hinnom Valley to be burned (today's Dung Gate, the lowest part of the walled city and natural exit of surface drainage, opens toward the same area). Over time, the Hebrew name of this valley, *ge bene-hinnom*, was shortened to *gehenna*. By intertestamental times, *gehenna* was used to refer to a place of fiery judgment reserved for the wicked (2 Esdras 7:36; cp. Matt. 5:22).

10 ▶ JERUSALEM IN THE TIME OF DAVID AND SOLOMON

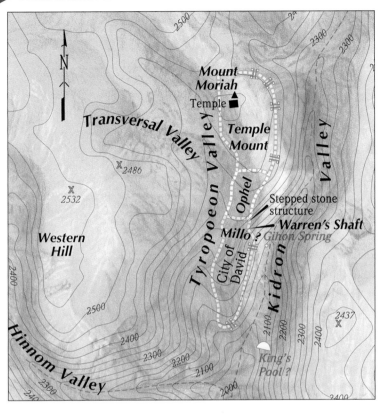

A smaller valley—today usually called the Central Valley, although it was known to Josephus as the Tyropoeon Valley or "Valley of the Cheesemakers"—divides the hill lying between the Kidron and Hinnom into two parts, a smaller, eastern hill and a larger, higher western hill. Settlement in Jerusalem began on the southern end of this eastern hill, above the Gihon Spring. A second, less powerful spring, En-rogel, lies further down the Kidron Valley (1 Kings 1:9, 43-45).

David's city, about 12 acres in size, encompassed only the southern end of the eastern hill (2 Sam. 5:6-10; 1 Chron. 21:18-30) (see Map 5). His son, Solomon, built the temple on the higher extension of this hill to the north (1 Kings 6:1-38; cp. 1 Chron. 22:1). Over the course of the next 200 years, houses were built on the western hill as the city's population slowly grew. Hezekiah enclosed the western hill by a massive wall in the late eighth century B.C. in response to the Assyrian threat against his kingdom (2 Chron. 32:5). The Bible calls this area of the city the *Mishneh* ("Second" or "New Quarter," 2 Kings 22:14; Zeph. 1:10).

The elevation of the hill on which David's Jerusalem and Solomon's temple were built is lower than that of the surrounding hills (i.e., the Mount of Olives, the western hill and the hills to the north and south). This fact was not lost on the Psalmist, who clearly knew the topography of Jerusalem when he wrote of the city under siege, "I raise my eyes toward the mountains. Where will my help come from? My help comes from the LORD, the Maker of heaven and earth" (Ps. 121:1-2). But mountains around the city can also shelter and protect: "the mountains surround her. And the LORD surrounds His people, both now and forever" (Ps. 125:2).

▲ The Mount of Olives viewed from the Temple Mount.

After the destruction of Jerusalem by Babylon, the city was restricted to the eastern hill, only to gradually grow during the centuries between the Testaments to again include the western hill and northern extension of the Tyropoeon Valley. The most significant change to Jerusalem by New Testament times, however, was the 35-acre artificial platform built over the Temple Mount and graced by a magnificently rebuilt temple. This massive engineering feat was accomplished under the sponsorship of Herod the Great, although he probably incorporated earlier Hasmonean elements into his project. The extent and function of the so-called "Third Wall" north of the New Testament city remains a matter of debate; many scholars attribute at least parts of it to Herod Agrippa I (A.D. 41–44), who apparently began to incorporate the northern hills (the "Bezetha") into the walled city. The Romans destroyed the entire city in A.D. 70.

The hills and valleys of Jerusalem determined the shape and character of the city over time as well as its natural limit of settlement. The city's topography was well known by the biblical writers, who incorporated images of its terrain in their divine message.

11 ▶ JERUSALEM IN THE NEW TESTAMENT PERIOD

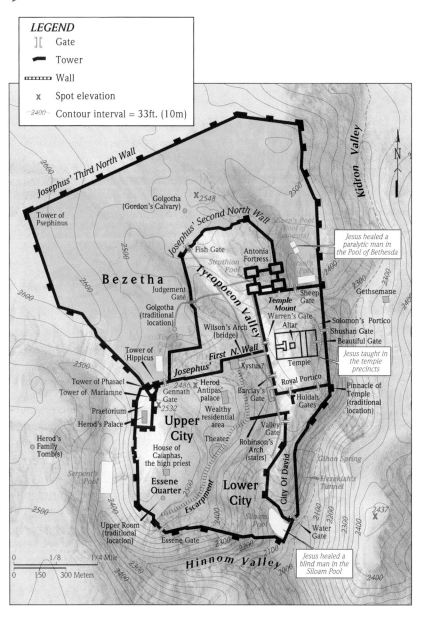

LEGEND
-][Gate
- ⬭ Tower
- ⬛⬛⬛ Wall
- x Spot elevation
- *—2400—* Contour interval = 33ft. (10m)

Kidron Valley

Josephus' Third North Wall

Golgotha
(Gordon's Calvary)   x2548

Josephus' Second North Wall

Tower of
Psephinus

Fish Gate   Antonia
Fortress

Jesus healed a
paralytic man in
the Pool of Bethesda

Sheep's Pool
(Pool of
Bethesda)

Struthion
Pool

Israel's
Pool

Bezetha

Judgement
Gate

Golgotha
(traditional
location)

Tyropoeon Valley

Sheep
Gate

**Temple
Mount**

Warren's Gate
Altar

Gethsemane

Solomon's Portico

Shushan Gate

Beautiful Gate

Wilson's Arch
(bridge)

Tower
Pool

First N. Wall

Josephus'

Xystus?

Temple

Jesus taught in
the temple
precincts

Tower of
Hippicus

Tower of Phasael
Tower of Mariamne

2486 x

Herod
Antipas'
palace

Gennath
Gate   x2532

Barclay's
Gate

Royal Portico

Pinnacle of
Temple
(traditional
location)

Huldah
Gates

Praetorium

Wealthy
residential
area

**Upper
City**

Herod's Palace

Valley
Gate

Herod's
Family
Tomb(s)

House of
Caiaphas,
the high priest

Theater

Robinson's
Arch
(stairs)

Gihon Spring

Serpent's
Pool

**Essene
Quarter**

Escarpment

**Lower
City**

Hezekiah's
Tunnel

2437
x

Upper Room
(traditional
location)

Essene Gate

Siloam
Pool

Water
Gate

City Of David

Hinnom Valley

Jesus healed a
blind man in the
Siloam Pool

N

0   1/8   1X4 Mile
0   150   300 Meters

THE CENTRAL REGIONS
(Israel/Samaria)

The central portion of Palestine generally corresponds to the heartland of the Northern Kingdom of Israel and the territory of New Testament Samaria. It is composed of five distinct geographical regions: the Hill Country of Ephraim, the Hill Country of Manasseh (Samaria), the Sharon Plain, Mount Carmel and the Jordan Valley.

12▶ PLAIN OF DOR, PLAIN OF SHARON, SAMARIA, JORDAN VALLEY, AND GILEAD

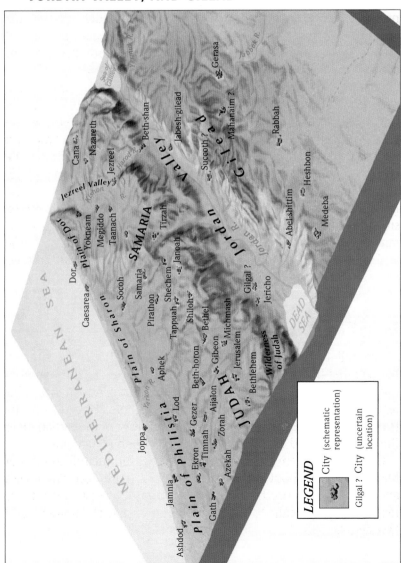

The Hill Country of Ephraim

The hill country of Ephraim is a rugged area of hard Cenomanian limestone lying north of the tribal inheritance of Benjamin. The region is 15 miles south to north, from Bethel to the Wadi Kanah (Josh. 16:8; 17:9-10), and stretches 27 miles east-west, from the Jordan Valley to the Plain of Sharon. The hill country of Ephraim thus corresponds to the heartland of the tribal territory of Ephraim (Josh. 16:1-10). The high point of the hill country of Ephraim is the hill of Baal-hazor (2 Sam. 13:23), 3,333 feet in elevation, located five miles northeast of Bethel.

The hills of Ephraim are well watered, receiving up to 30 inches of rain annually in regions west of the watershed ridge. This, plus the numerous small springs that dot the wadis, provides ample water resources for agriculture. Like the hill country of Judah, the hills of Ephraim are terraced, and their rich terra rosa soil provides excellent crops of grapes, figs, olives, pomegranates and almonds.

The main center of the hill country of Ephraim during the biblical period was Shiloh, tucked among the hills in the upper reaches of the Nahal Shiloh just west of the watershed ridge. Small but broad valleys in the vicinity of Shiloh provide a nice agricultural base, and its relative seclusion made this a natural center for the ark of the covenant while Israel settled the land (Josh. 18:1; 21:1-3; Judg. 21:12, 19-23; 1 Sam. 1:3; 4:1-4). Shiloh was a large walled city during the middle Bronze II Age (18th through 16th centuries B.C.) but only a small village during the time of the judges. Because of its rugged terrain, the hill country of Ephraim is largely closed to outside traffic and cultural influences. This is a land of farms and small villages, well suited to the agricultural life of ancient Israel.

The Hill Country of Manasseh

The hill country of Manasseh is a large hilly region situated between the hill country of Ephraim and the Jezreel Valley, approximately 32 miles east-west and 22 miles north-south in size. This region generally corresponds to the heartland of the portion of the tribal territory that was allotted to Manasseh west of the Jordan River (Josh. 17:7-10) and to the New Testament region of Samaria.

Geologically, there are three sub-regions within the hill country of Manasseh, each about the size and shape of the Judean Shephelah and each oriented north-northeast by south-southwest. Today these regions are often called "Eastern Samaria," "Central Samaria," and "Western Samaria."

The two highest hills in all of Manasseh, Mount Ebal (3,084 feet) and Mount Gerazim (2,891 feet) (Deut. 11:29-30; Josh. 8:30-35) dominate the southern end of Central Samaria, while the northern end terminates in Mount Gilboa (1,600 feet; 1 Sam. 31:1-8). Central Samaria is separated from Eastern Samaria by a narrow chalk depression forming a direct natural link between Shechem and Beth-shan (1 Sam. 31:12). Central Samaria receives approximately 20–25 inches of rainfall per year.

Mount Ebal lies near the ancient city of Shechem.

The broad valleys, relatively gentle hills, good soil, and adequate rainfall of Manasseh give shape to a land where shepherds and farmers, grain fields and orchards all thrive. This mixed economy provides a stable economic base for the region, allowing its inhabitants to live and prosper off the land.

The city of Shechem (modern Nablus), located at the head of Nahal Shechem between Mounts Ebal and Gerazim, is the natural center of Manasseh. Historically Shechem was also the natural "capital" of the entire hill country, the point from which kingdoms and would-be kingdoms radiated throughout central Palestine (cp. Gen. 33:18–34:31; Judg. 9:1-57; 1 Kings 12:1,25; cp. Josh. 8:30-35). Unlike Jerusalem, Shechem's geographical position is open and inviting. Valleys carrying natural routes extend from Shechem in four directions—toward the east, south toward Bethel and Jerusalem, northwest through Nahal Shechem to the coast, and northeast to Beth-shean with a side route down the Wadi Faria to the Jordan Valley. While these valleys provide Shechem with a strong agricultural base, they also open the region to easy invasion.

Jeroboam, the first king of the Northern Kingdom of Israel, established his capital at Shechem (1 Kings 12:25).

Mount Gilboa.

Later in his reign, and perhaps as a defensive measure to protect his kingdom against pressures from the south and west, Jeroboam moved his capital to Tirzah, a city nestled in the chalk pass connecting Shechem with Beth-shean at the head of the Wadi Faria (1 Kings 14:17; 15:21,33; 16:15). From this relatively isolated position, Jeroboam was able to consolidate his kingdom's holdings in Gilead to the east (Transjordan). A generation later, Omri, the father of Ahab, moved the capital again, this time to Samaria (1 Kings 16:23-24,29), a prominent hill in Nahal Shechem with easy access to the coast, where it remained until the destruction of the Northern Kingdom (2 Kings 17:1-6). From Samaria, the Israelite kings were able to expand their influence to Phoenicia and the coast (cp. 1 Kings 16:31).

Following common practice in the ancient Near Eastern world, biblical writers often used "Samaria," the name of the capital city of Israel, to refer to the entire Northern Kingdom (cp. 1 Kings 13:32; 2 Kings 17:24; Jer. 23:13; Hos.10:7). "Samaria" also became the official name of the Assyrian province in central Palestine after the fall of Israel to Sargon II in 722 B.C. The name was maintained for the region throughout the time of the New Testament (e.g., John 4:4) and is commonly used by Israelis for the region today.

Long colonnaded street built by the emperor Severus at NT Sebaste which was the OT city of Samaria.

The city of Samaria was a thriving Hellenistic city in the third and second centuries B.C. before it was destroyed by John Hyrcanus, the Hasmonean Jewish king and nationalist, in 106 B.C. Herod the Great rebuilt the city and renamed it Sebaste, the Greek form of "Augustus," in honor of his emperor in Rome. Here Herod settled foreign mercenaries who had helped him put down resistance from Jewish nationalists at the beginning of his reign. On the high point of the site, over the ruins of Ahab's palace, Herod built a magnificent white limestone temple that he dedicated to Caesar Augustus.

The hill country of Manasseh—New Testament Samaria—is a blessed land with easy access to the world beyond. Ancient Israel grew rich here—and complacent. With barbed words, the Prophets Amos and Hosea laid bare the self-centered people of this land, who serve as a warning for people who live in similar conditions today.

The Plain of Sharon

The portion of the coastal plain between Mount Carmel and the Yarkon River is known as the Plain of Sharon (1 Chron. 5:16). The northern boundary of the Sharon is actually Nahal Tanninim (the Crocodile River), a small stream flowing westward from the Mount Carmel range to the Mediterranean Sea. The Plain of Sharon is approximately 10 miles wide and 30 miles long and rises only slightly to the western foothills of Manasseh.

Like the Philistine coastal plain to the south, the Plain of Sharon is primarily composed of sand mixed with alluvial soils that have washed down from the eastern hills. Along the coast, three parallel ridges of solidified sand (*kurkar*) block the flow of water from the hills forming swamps that impede agriculture. When drained, as today, the Sharon is an agricultural breadbasket, particularly well suited for citrus.

Because of its sandy swamps, the Plain of Sharon of antiquity was home to an exuberant fertility of scrub and oak forests, undergrowth and wildflowers (cp. Song 2:1). Like the heights of Mount Carmel, Lebanon, and Bashan, the Plain of Sharon was famous for its wild

▲ View of the Plain of Sharon and the Yarkon River from the excavation area at the site of Aphek.

vegetation and natural grazing land (cp. 1 Chron. 27:29). The biblical writers used the fertility of the Sharon to signal God's blessing on a renewed earth (Isa. 35:1-2; 65:10; cp. Isa. 33:9).

During most of the biblical period, no sizeable towns or harbors of any consequence bent the international highway to the shore as it traversed the Plain of Sharon. Only in the first century did Herod the Great begin to build the magnificent port city of Caesarea there (Acts 10:1-8; 23:23-24,31-33), destined by late Roman times to become the largest port in the eastern Mediterranean.

Herod's port at Caesarea was intended to show the world that the King of Judea could do the impossible. Using huge wooden frames weighted and sunk by stone, then secured by cement that could harden underwater, Herod's workmen built a massive harbor extending 650 feet from the stiff coastline into the sea. Herod's choice of the northern Sharon coast for a harbor may have been a mirror of his megalomania, but it was also a stroke of genius; for from this spot he was able to control international traffic into both Judea and Galilee.

Because of its sandy swamps and stiff coastline, the Plain of Sharon did not figure prominently in the Old Testament story. By the time of the New Testament, however, the port of Caesarea had taken hold of the coast, and from here the Apostle Paul launched the gospel to the Mediterranean world.

Mount Carmel

The Mount Carmel range is one of the most prominent topographical features of Palestine. The range rises abruptly from the coastal plain and Jezreel Valley, jutting dramatically into the Mediterranean; its promontory gives the coastline its characteristic "hook" shape. Oriented sharply northwest-southeast and at right angles to the main line of hills in western Palestine, the Carmel range is composed of three distinct geological regions.

Mount Carmel range.

The Mediterranean Sea as seen through the arches of the Herodian aquaduct at Caesarea. It was from this port that Paul launched the gospel to the Greco-Roman world.

The name "Carmel" means "plantation," or "garden-land," and is quite appropriate for the verdant Carmel range. The natural fertility, beauty, and strength of Carmel was an object of admiration for the biblical poets (Song 7:5; Isa. 35:1-2; Jer. 50:19). With powerful imagery, they often compared God's withering judgment to the summit of Carmel drying up—a sign of doom indeed! (Isa. 33:9; Amos 1:2; Nah. 1:4).

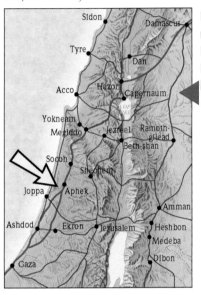

Northeast of the Mount Carmel range it is more proper to speak simply of the International Highway rather than the International Coastal Highway, since from here the route no longer follows the coast.

Because of its inaccessibility, Mount Carmel proper has tended to be a place of refuge and escape (cp. Amos 9:3). Its majestic, wooded height is also a natural setting for religious sanctuary. Egyptian records from Thutmose III, Ramses II, and Ramses III (15th–12th centuries B.C.) call Mount Carmel "the Holy Headland," suggesting it was thought to be a place of divine abode from early times. A document from the fourth century B.C. calls Carmel "the holy mountain of Zeus." Mount Carmel was also held in high esteem by the indigenous nature-based fertility religion of Canaan. When Elijah chose to challenge the prophets of Baal, the Canaanite god of lightning and rain, on Mount Carmel, he deliberately entered Baal's "home court," making his victory all the more decisive (1 Kings 18:16-46). The prophet Elisha frequented Mount Carmel a generation later (2 Kings 2:25; 4:25).

Mount Carmel is a prominent marker on both the physical landscape of Palestine and the religious landscape of the Old Testament story. Here the LORD showed that He is God of all creation and that even places of abundant rainfall will wither at His command.

The Jordan Valley

The Jordan Valley is the portion of the rift valley that lies between the Sea of Galilee and the Dead Sea. The valley itself is only 65 miles long, but the Jordan River, meandering a torturous path to the Dead Sea, is approximately 135 miles in length. The entire valley lies below sea level, dropping gradually from -690 feet at the Sea of Galilee to -1,350 feet at the Dead Sea.

The Jordan Valley varies in width from 2 to 15 miles, with the broadest portion in the south, just above the Dead Sea. Here the Bible speaks of the "plains of Jericho" (Josh. 4:13; 2 Kings 25:5) west of the Jordan, and the "plains of Moab" east of the river (Num. 26:3; Deut. 34:1). In the north, just over 10 miles below the Sea of Galilee, the valley also widens considerably to the west. This extension of the

Jordan Valley.

Jordan Valley is commonly called the Beth-shean Valley, after the city of Beth-shean on its northern edge. The Beth-shean Valley provides an important connection with the Jezreel Valley further west.

In speaking of the unique character of the Jordan Valley, the historical geographer George Adam Smith has commented, "There may be something on the surface of another planet to match the Jordan Valley; there is nothing on this" (*The Historical Geography of the Holy Land*, Hodder & Stoughton, 1931, p. 301). Describing the actual trench cut by the Jordan, Smith notes, "the Jordan sweeps to the Dead Sea through unhealthy jungle relieved only by poisonous soil" (p. 313).

 The Jordan River flows south from Mount Hermon through Israel, finally emptying into the Dead Sea.

The climate of the Jordan Valley changes dramatically in its 65-mile course from the Sea of Galilee to the Dead Sea. The north enjoys a Mediterranean climate, with rainfall of 18 inches per year. Fifteen miles south, the valley around Beth-shean has an arid steppe climate (12 inches of rain per year), while the southern Jordan Valley is desert (4 inches of rain annually).

Although natural routes run the length of the Jordan Valley on both sides of the river, the preferred route of antiquity was on the east, following the line of springs at the scarp of the Transjordanian hills. It was this route that Jesus most often traveled on His journeys between Galilee and Jerusalem. The primary fords crossing the Jordan are at Jericho, Adam (the outlet of the Wadi Faria; Josh. 3:16), and points near Beth-shean. These crossings carry important east-west routes that tie western Palestine to Transjordan. In spite of the heat and difficulty of travel, the Jordan Valley has always been a rather permeable border for peoples who live on either side (cp. Gen. 33:16-18; Deut. 9:1; Josh. 3:1-17; 22:1-34; Judg. 3:12-13; 7:24; 12:1-6; 21:8-12; 2 Sam. 17:21-22).

Elisha received the mantle of power and authority from Elijah after both had crossed to the eastern side of the Jordan Valley (2 Kings 2:1-14). Jesus was baptized, receiving power and authority from on high, in the Jordan Valley (Matt. 3:1-17; Mark 1:9-13; Luke 3:21-22). Traditions vary as to whether Jesus was baptized on the east or west bank of the Jordan or in the northern or southern part of the valley. Regardless, His baptism in the Jordan has provided a rich motif for Christian art and hymnody throughout the centuries.

Except for some cities in the north and the oasis of Jericho, few people settled in the Jordan Valley in antiquity. Many biblical characters crossed the valley, however, in spite of its wild and harsh conditions. The Jordan became an important symbol in Christian art and theology, signaling barriers (such as death) that we can only cross with God's help.

▲ The Jordan River just north of the Sea of Galilee.

THE NORTHERN REGIONS
(Galilee)

The northern portion of Palestine, called Galilee in both the Old and New Testaments, is composed of five distinct geographical regions: the Jezreel Valley, Lower Galilee, Upper Galilee, the Sea of Galilee and the Huleh Basin (see map 4, p.13).

13► NORTHERN COASTAL PLAINS, JEZREEL VALLEY, GALILEE AND BASHAN

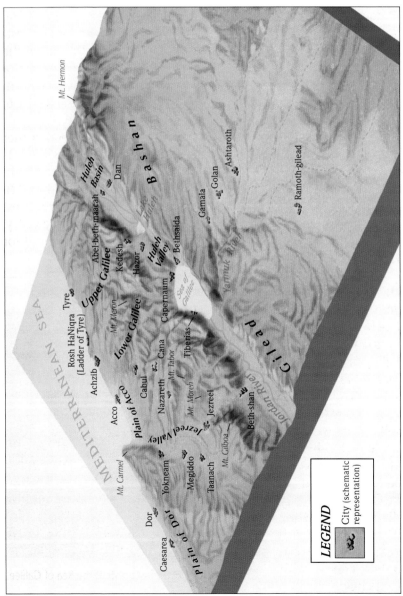

LEGEND
City (schematic representation)

The Jezreel Valley

The Jezreel Valley is the largest and most fertile valley in Palestine. It is shaped roughly like the head of a spear with its "point" facing northwest toward the Mediterranean. The "shaft" of the spearhead, the narrow Harod Valley, leads southeast to Beth-shean and the Jordan Valley. Together, the Jezreel and Harod Valleys are the land's most important international crossroads.

▲ The Valley of Jezreel (or Esdraelon or Megiddo) as viewed from the top of the Megiddo tel.

"Jezreel" means "God sows," which is certainly a fitting name for the valley that is Palestine's breadbasket. Besides the name "Valley of Jezreel" (Josh. 17:16; Judg. 6:33; Hos. 1:5), the Bible also calls this region "the plain of Megiddo" (Zech. 12:11) and, poetically, "the pasturelands of God" (Ps. 83:12). The term "Esdraelon" is a Greek form of "Jezreel" occurring only in extrabiblical literature from the New Testament period. "Armageddon" (Rev. 16:16) is a Greek word that has long been assumed to render the Hebrew phrase *har Megiddo*, "the mountain of Megiddo"; it is usually understood as referring to the entire Jezreel Valley.

Jerome Murphy-O'Connor has characterized Megiddo as "the royal box in one of the great theatres of history. From time immemorial armies have surged from the surrounding valleys to play their parts on the flat stage of the Jezreel valley" (Jerome Murphy-O'Connor, *The Holy Land*, 4th ed., New York: Oxford, 1998, p. 342). The Bible records several military actions that took place in the Jezreel and Harod Valleys. These include the battle of Deborah and Barak against Sisera (Judg. 4–5); the battle of Gideon against the Midianites (Judg. 7); Saul's last stand against the Philistines (1 Sam.

28:4; 31:1-10); Jehu's *coup d'etat* (2 Kings 9:14-37); and Josiah's attempted facedown of Pharaoh Neco (2 Kings 23:28-30).

The mountains that surround the Jezreel Valley contrast sharply with the low, open expanse of the valley itself. The Jezreel is drained toward the Mediterranean by the Nahal Kishon, which collects runoff rainfall from the surrounding hills. Because of the flatness of the Jezreel, the size of its runoff area, and the narrowness of the pass at the foot of Mount Carmel through which the valley drains, a heavy rainstorm will turn the valley floor into a soggy, muddy morass. Wintertime conditions have impeded armies, chariots, and travelers throughout history (cp. Judg. 4:13-15; 5:19-21; 1 Kings 18:45-46). To the east, the valley floor dips below sea level at the point where the Harod Valley joins the Jezreel, then drops gradually into the rift. The Harod is drained by the Nahal Harod. Several powerful springs line the foot of Mount Gilboa along its southern edge (Judg. 7:1).

The rich alluvial soil of the Jezreel Valley is as much as 330 feet deep in places, and the abundance of water ensures excellent crops even in years of limited rainfall. The agriculture possibilities here are so extraordinary compared to the rest of Palestine that Herod the Great claimed the valley as his own royal estate. Today the Jezreel is drained and fertile fields abound.

Because of the muddy wintertime conditions, the Jezreel's natural routes generally follow the perimeter of the Valley. The exception is the International Coastal Highway. An underground rise of basalt has slightly raised the level of the valley floor on a line running between Megiddo and Mount Tabor. In antiquity the International Highway followed this low ridge across the Jezreel as it began to pick its way through the natural obstacles of Galilee to Damascus.

The Jezreel Valley has always been the major crossroads of Palestine. Here the main International Highway crosses a second that connects the Plain of Acco to the Jordan Valley and Transjordanian Highway beyond. The ceaseless flow of travelers and armies through the Jezreel via these international highways gave rise to the biblical phrase "Galilee of the Gentiles" (Isa. 9:1; Matt. 4:15).

Because of its superior farmland and strategic highways, the Jezreel Valley has always been one of the most valuable pieces of real estate in Palestine. Overflowing with material blessings, this valley was Israel's testing ground of faith. Perhaps for this reason it figures so prominently in John's Apocalypse (Rev. 16:16).

Lower Galilee

Lower Galilee is an area of relatively open topography that lies north of the Jezreel and Harod Valleys and between the Mediterranean Sea and rift valley. In size, Lower Galilee measures 25 miles east-west and between 15 and 30 miles north-south. "Lower" Galilee is not a biblical name but a convenient way to refer to that portion of Galilee that is lower in elevation (below 2,000 feet) and hence more open to travel than the more mountainous region further north.

Lower Galilee can be divided into three distinct geological regions: the Plain of Acco, western Lower Galilee, and eastern Lower Galilee.

The east-west valleys of western Lower Galilee act as a type of wind tunnel, channeling the westerly afternoon breezes off the Mediterranean directly toward the Sea of Galilee. The winds gain strength through these "tunnels" and drop dramatically into the rift, where they bang up against the steep scarp of hills on the eastern side of the sea. If the winds pick up suddenly, they can quickly turn the low, relatively shallow Sea of Galilee into a churning mass of water. This evidently happened to Jesus and His disciples one night as they made their way across the sea in a small boat: "A fierce windstorm arose, and the waves were breaking over the boat, so that the boat was already being swamped" (Mark 4:37). Jesus calmed the sea as He would a baby, and His disciples were understandably incredulous (Mark 4:38-41).

 A storm breaking across the Sea of Galilee.

The relatively low terrain and broad valleys of Lower Galilee make for fairly easy travel. The International Highway enters Lower Galilee from the south at Mount Tabor, then angles to the Sea of Galilee by following a topographical line formed by the "seam" between the limestone hills of western Lower Galilee and the basalt hills of eastern Lower Galilee. On the way, it skirts the Horns of Hattin, the extinct and eroded volcanic cone that was responsible for the basalt in the region. The International Highway then drops to the Sea of Galilee through the narrow Arbel pass, a sheer cut in the basalt ridge that boarders the sea on the southwest. The top of the cliff above this pass provides a breathtaking sweep of Galilee, from Mount Tabor to snowy Mount Hermon north of Bashan.

The International Highway from Aphek to Damascus.

A second major natural route in Lower Galilee connects Acco/Ptolemais to Tiberius on the western shore of the Sea of Galilee, passing through the broad Valley of Iphtah-el on the way. This route was Galilee's lifeline to the world during the time of the New Testament, tying the mixed population Galilee to the Greco-Roman lands of the Mediterranean.

The capital of Galilee during Jesus' early years was Sepphoris, a Greco-Roman city in the Valley of Iphtah-el just over five miles north of Nazareth. Sepphoris had been captured by Jewish nationalists following the death of Herod the Great in 4 B.C., then burned as Roman troops dislodged the Jews from the city. Herod Antipas, son of Herod the Great and his successor as king in Galilee, began to rebuild Sepphoris a year later. Jesus' father, Joseph, a skilled workman in wood and stone (Gk. *tekton*, Mark 6:3), may have helped to rebuild Sepphoris as jobs were probably scarce in his small, poor hometown. Jesus may have honed His skills as a craftsman in Sepphoris as well.

Because of its openness, good soil, and pleasant climate, Lower Galilee has always been a favored region for settlement. This was a prize coveted by the kings of ancient Israel but separated from the Israelite heartland by the wide-open (and militarily dangerous) Jezreel Valley.

Mount Tabor, located a few miles southeast of Nazareth.

Throughout history, ancient Israel had trouble holding on to Galilee. Isaiah spoke of "Galilee of the Gentiles" (Isa. 9:1) as all Galilee was being cut off by a ruthless Assyrian army, sweeping down the International Highway from the northeast. Galilee was no less a region of Gentile influence in the first century, when Jesus used Isaiah's words to introduce a kingdom that far surpasses the work of even the greatest armies and kings (Matt. 4:15).

Repeated cultural and military threats by Canaanites, Phoenicians, Syrians, Greeks, and Romans throughout the biblical period caused many Jews living in Galilee in Jesus' day to adopt a strongly nationalistic stance against the world around them. This attitude probably led the men of Nazareth to try to kill Jesus when He preached that God's favor rested also on Galilee's Gentile neighbors (Luke 4:16-30). On another occasion, the Pharisees declared that Jesus couldn't be the Messiah because no prophet had ever come from Galilee (John 7:40-52). They failed to mention that Jonah, the prophet whom God had sent to Israel's worst enemy, the Assyrians, was also from Galilee (2 Kings 14:25). Not insignificantly, Jonah's hometown, Gath-hepher, lay only five miles from Nazareth.

Lower Galilee is blessed with many natural resources: good water and soil, an agreeable climate, important highways, and pleasant vistas. This was the boyhood homeland of Jesus—and here He grew up, hearing the great stories of His peoples' struggles for redemption through the ages. The openness of Galilee provided the stimulating environment in which Jesus first began to preach a new kind of kingdom.

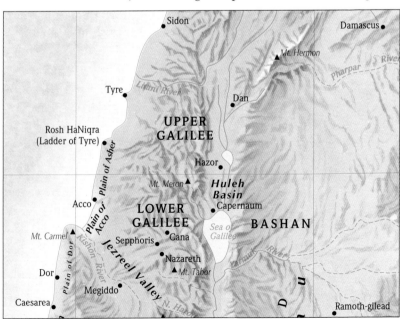

Lower and Upper Galilee.

Upper Galilee

Upper Galilee is the rugged, uplifted limestone region north of Lower Galilee. The eastern boundary is a steep scarp above the Huleh Basin (the upper Jordan Valley), while on the west, the hills drop to the Plain of Acco and into the Mediterranean Sea. To the north, Upper Galilee rises gradually to the mountainous Lebanese Range, beyond the Litani River. Hard Cenomanian limestone dominates the western two-thirds of Upper Galilee, while the eastern third is primarily softer Eocene limestone.

Numerous small fault lines have dissected the topography of Upper Galilee, breaking the landform into rugged, uneven blocks. The high point is Mount Meron, slightly southeast of center. At 3,963 feet, Meron is also the highest point in all of western Palestine. Deep wadis cut away from Mount Meron in every direction, adding to the region's rugged topography.

The high elevation and northwestern exposure of Upper Galilee ensures abundant rainfall, up to 40 inches or more annually. The soil is fertile, and natural scrub forests blanket the hills with green throughout the year. For ancient Israel, Upper Galilee was a taste of the richness of Lebanon, so often a symbol of strength and fertility in the biblical texts (e.g., Pss. 29:5-6; 92:12; Song 4:15; 5:15; Isa. 60:13; Jer. 18:14).

Because of its ruggedness, Upper Galilee has never been a region of large cities. Rather, numerous small towns and villages dotted the landscape in antiquity, just as they do today. Natural routes tend to avoid Upper Galilee, adding to its remoteness. Joshua allotted the western portion of Upper Galilee, along with the Plain of Acco, to the tribe of Asher (Josh. 19:24-31), and the higher, eastern portion to Naphtali (Josh. 19:32-39). Here Israel could dwell in safety, away from the strong Canaanite presence in the valleys to the west, south, and east. Archaeological evidence has uncovered the remains of many small settlement villages in Upper Galilee dating to the 13th–11th centuries B.C. (Iron I), the time of ancient Israel's settlement in the land.

The blessings that Jacob bestowed on his 12 sons are reflected in the actual territories in which the 12 tribes of Israel eventually settled. For instance, Jacob blessed Naphtali by saying, "Naphtali is a doe set free that bears beautiful fawns" (Gen. 49:21 NIV). This short blessing evokes vivid images of a wild and beautiful land, where Israel could live in freedom and safety. Moses' blessing on the tribe of Naphtali echoes Jacob's: "Naphtali is abounding with the favor of the LORD and is full of his blessing; he will inherit southward to the lake [i.e., the Sea of Galilee]" (Deut. 33:23).

During the time of the New Testament, Upper Galilee was filled with small, largely conservative farming villages. Jesus no doubt visited some of them on His journey from the Sea of Galilee to Phoenicia (Matt. 15:21-28). In the second century A.D., after the Jews had been banished from Jerusalem by Rome, Jewish life flourished in the remote hills of Upper Galilee, away from the hassles and temptations of the valleys and plains below. Zefat (Safed), the primary city of Upper Galilee today, was an important center of Jewish learning in the medieval period.

The rugged limestone hills of Upper Galilee allow a similar lifestyle as is found in the hill country of Judah and Ephraim. Here ancient Israel felt at home, even though separated from the southern tribes by a wide "international" zone that was usually overrun by Gentiles.

The Sea of Galilee

The Sea of Galilee as viewed from the northwest.

The Sea of Galilee fills a shallow depression in the rift valley east of Lower Galilee. The Jordan River enters the sea from the northeast and exits to the southwest. The surface of the sea is 690 feet below sea level, and its bottom lies 150 feet below that. The sea measures just 13 by 7 miles, more a lake than a sea.

The Sea of Galilee is known by several names in the Bible: the Sea of Chinnereth (Num. 34:11; Deut. 3:17; Josh. 12:3; 13:27), the Lake of Gennesaret (Luke 5:1), the Sea of Tiberius (John 6:1; 21:1), the Sea of Galilee (Matt. 4:18; 15:29; Mark 1:16; 7:31), and simply the "sea" or "lake" (e.g., Matt. 8:24). Some believe that the name Chinnereth, which is perhaps related to the Hebrew word for "harp," derives from the sea's harp shape. More likely, the sea was simply named after the city of Chinnereth, located on its northwestern shore during Old Testament times (Josh. 19:35). Gennesaret is a form of Chinnereth. Today Israelis call the Sea of Galilee "the Kinneret."

The sea is enclosed by basalt hills that rise 1,300 feet above the surface of the water (approximately 600 feet above sea level). To the east and west, the scarp of the rift valley presses close to the sea, while on the north, the remains of a huge flow of basalt (the Rosh Pinna sill) separates the sea from the Huleh Basin. Three plains provide fertile fields for agriculture: the Plain of Bethsaida to the northeast where the Jordan enters the sea, the Plain of Gennesaret on the northwest (cp. Matt. 14:34-36), and a plain formed by the Jordan Valley to the south.

The Sea of Galilee receives less rainfall than the surrounding hills, about 16 inches annually. Temperatures are moderate to hot, and the air is usually humid. Several hot mineral springs enter the Sea of Galilee from its shore and bottom, a result of the gigantic rip in the surface of the earth that formed the rift valley. Fish tend to congregate around these springs in the wintertime. Many fish are also found in the northeast, feeding on the organic matter deposited into the sea by the Jordan River. Fishing and agriculture are excellent, as the Gospel writers did attest.

The New Testament mentions three different kinds of fishing nets that were used in the Sea of Galilee. A cast net was a circular net 25 feet in diameter with sinkers around the edge; it was cast into shallow water by a fisherman standing near shore (Mark 1:16-18). The dragnet or seine was 800–900 feet long, 12–25 feet wide and weighted along one edge. This net was unrolled by boat into a huge arc and stood upright in the water. It was then drawn ashore by fisherman standing at the water's edge. Because the dragnet pulled everything within its arc to shore (cp. Hab. 1:15), the fish it caught had to be sorted for commercial viability (Matt. 13:47-48). A trammel net consisted of a cross-netting of three nets. Because fish easily caught their gills in its web, trammel nets had to be repaired often (Mark 1:19-20). A fishhook is mentioned only once in the Gospels (Matt. 17:24-27).

Jesus' ministry was focused on the northern shore of the Sea of Galilee. He made His home in Capernaum (Matt. 4:12-17; 9:1) and called His disciples from villages in the vicinity (Matt. 4:18-22). At least three disciples, Philip, Peter, and Andrew, hailed from Bethsaida (John 1:44). Although its exact location remains in doubt, Bethsaida was apparently either in the marshy delta of the Jordan (el-Araj) or on a higher mound slightly north (et-Tell). A third town visited often by Jesus, Chorazin, was located in the basalt hills (the Rosh Pinna sill) above Capernaum (Matt. 11:21). It was probably in these hills that Jesus went in the early mornings to find "a deserted place" to pray (Mark 1:35).

"Its nature is wonderful as well as its beauty. Its soil is so fruitful that all sorts of trees can grow upon it, and the inhabitants accordingly plant all sorts of trees there, for the temper of the air is so well mixed that it agrees very well with all. One may call this place the ambition of nature, where it forces those plants that are naturally enemies to one another to agree together. It supplies men with the principle fruits, with grapes and figs continually, during 10 months in the year and the rest of the fruit as it becomes ripe together, through the whole year, for besides the good temperature of the air, it is also watered from a most fertile spring. The people of the country call it Capernaum" (Josephus, Wars iii.10.8).

The local building material around the Sea of Galilee is hard, black basaltic stone. Archaeological excavations have uncovered square blocks of houses (*insulae*) built of this stone in Capernaum, Bethsaida, Chorazin, and other villages in the region. The rooms in these houses were small and dark, with low doors and narrow windows set high in the wall above. One such *insula* excavated in Capernaum is believed to have belonged to Peter (Mark 1:29-30), where Jesus apparently made His home. The synagogue in Capernaum in Jesus' day was also made of black basaltic stone. The white synagogue that dominates Capernaum today was built in a later century out of Cenomanian limestone brought from the hills of Lower Galilee.

An overview of the third-century synagogue at Capernaum.

Capernaum is often thought of as a sleepy fishing village, but during the first century it had a vibrant, mixed economy. In addition to fishing and agriculture (e.g., Mark 4:1-9), archaeological evidence suggests that Capernaum was also a place where high-quality agricultural implements were manufactured. Many olive presses and grain mills made out of local basalt, a highly durable and abrasive rock, were found in excavations at Capernaum, more, in fact, than the local population would have been expected to use by themselves. Because Capernaum was on a trade route and was the first village that travelers came to in Herod Antipas' Galilee after crossing the Jordan River from the east, Rome made it a tax collection center (cp. Mark 2:14-15). To enforce tax collection, a unit of Roman soldiers was also garrisoned in Capernaum (cp. Luke 7:2-5).

▲ The foundational material of this third-century synagogue may possibly date from the first century.

Three separate political entities bordered the Sea of Galilee in the first century A.D. (see Map 9). Galilee proper, governed by Herod Antipas, son of Herod the Great, was located west of the sea and Jordan River. The main city on the western Galilee shore was—and still is—Tiberius, founded by Antipas between A.D. 17 and 20 to honor the new Caesar in Rome. Tiberius is within sight of Capernaum and an easy two-hour walk away, yet the Gospels fail to mention if Jesus ever went there (but cp. John 6:23-24).

The territory lying east of the Jordan River and northeast of the Sea of Galilee was governed by Herod Philip, another son of Herod the Great. Philip's territory was divided into three expansive regions, Gaulanitus, Iturea, and Traconitis (cp. Luke 3:1,19). Philip raised Bethsaida, his main city on the sea, to the status of a Greco-Roman *polis*, renaming it Julius after the daughter of Caesar Augustus.

A confederation of 10 Greco-Roman cities called the Decapolis lay south of Philip's territory, stretching from the southeastern shore of the sea deep into Transjordan. This Gentile region was home to the Gerasenes, where Jesus healed a man possessed by demons (Mark 5:1-20). One of the Decapolis cities, Hippus, sat on a prominent hill above the Sea of Galilee within sight of Capernaum (cp. Matt. 5:14).

These various political regions in the New Testament period were closely connected by sea and land. Here people with every competing religious and political ideology and agenda were crowded together under tropical heat and the ever-watchful eye of Rome. It was in this pressure-cooker setting that Jesus chose to minister. Here He could touch the very human needs of influential people and commoner alike, of Jews, Gentiles, and persons torn between.

The Sea of Galilee was an ideal setting for the Gospel story. Here Jesus placed Himself in the center of all of the forces competing for power and influence in His day. Here He also met and ministered to "just regular folk," people who were searching how to live quiet lives that were pleasing to God and man.

14 ▶ THE MINISTRY OF JESUS AROUND THE SEA OF GALILEE

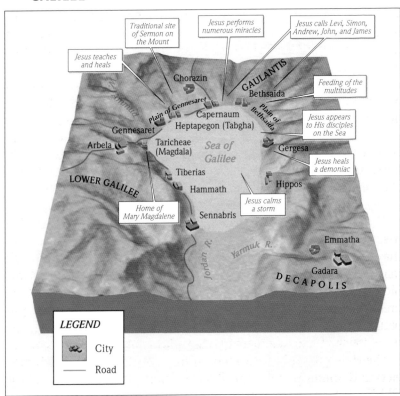

The Huleh Basin

The Huleh Basin is the northernmost extension of the Jordan Valley. The northern point of the basin, the city of Dan, lies 25 miles north of the Sea of Galilee, at the foothills of Mount Hermon. The southern end is "plugged" by the thick basalt Rosh Pinna sill, a lava flow from Bashan. The floor of the basin lies approximately 240 feet above sea level, requiring the Jordan River to drop considerably on its journey through a narrow cut in the eastern side of the sill to the Sea

The Huleh Basin.

of Galilee (-690 feet). The Cenomanian limestone hills of Upper Galilee tower 1,600 feet above the Huleh to the west, while the basalt slopes of Bashan pull back more gradually to the east.

The Huleh is filled with rich alluvial soil (basaltic and terra rosa) and some peat. In the north, rainfall reaches 25 inches per year. Most of the water in the basin, however, comes from the four tributaries of the Jordan River (Nahal Hermon, Nahal Dan, Nahal Senir, and Nahal Ijon), that produce a combined 5,000 gallons of water per second. These tributaries arise from huge karstic springs in the southern end of Mount Hermon and are fed year-round by snowmelt from its heights (cp. Jer. 18:14). Because of the steep sides of the basin, strong winds tend to skip over the top, while sunlight pours down. Together, the soil, water, and heat produce greenhouse-like conditions, and a wide variety of crops are grown year-round. Should one choose to do so, it is possible to get 18 cuttings of alfalfa in the basin per year.

The waters of the Jordan back up at the southern end of the Huleh Basin as they are slowed through the cut of the Rosh Pinna sill. Until the early 1950s these waters formed a small lake, Lake Huleh, with marshes, papyrus, and water birds common to the Nile Delta. Some Bible atlases suggest that this lake was the "Waters of Merom" that figured in Joshua's defeat of Hazor (Josh. 11:5), but others connect this battle with Mount Meron in Upper Galilee. Today, Lake Huleh has been drained for agriculture although a lush nature preserve remains.

The Huleh Basin has always been the funnel through which travelers and armies poured into Palestine from the north. During the Old Testament period, the International Highway passed through

Dan (Gen. 14:14; Judg. 18:27-29; 2 Sam. 3:10; 1 Kings 12:29) and skirted the western edge of the Huleh, out of its swampy soil, to Hazor (Josh. 11:1; Judg. 4:2; 1 Kings 9:15). It then crossed the Rosh Pinna sill to Chinnereth on the Sea of Galilee before finding its way through the natural obstacles of Galilee to the coast. In the time of the New Testament, however, the international route dropped down the eastern side of the basin, connecting Caesarea Philippi (Matt. 16:13), at the edge of the foothills of Mount Hermon, with Bethsaida-Julius on the Sea of Galilee.

The city of Hazor is mentioned several times in cuneiform tablets from the middle and late Bronze Ages (20th through 13th centuries B.C.), testifying to its importance as "the head of all these kingdoms" (Josh. 11:10). Archaeological excavations have corroborated Hazor's importance. On the eve of Joshua's conquest, the city was 200 acres in size, 10 times bigger than other Canaanite cities of the time and of a size rivaling the great cities of Mesopotamia. Recent excavations have uncovered remains of the grand Canaanite palace at Hazor, with rooms paneled in basalt. While a handful of cuneiform tablets have been found at Hazor, the city's full archive, which was probably housed in the palace, remains to be discovered.

 Israelite storehouses dating from the ninth century B.C. at ancient Hazor in Israel.

Because of its position astride the northern approaches of Palestine, the Huleh Basin is the land's first line of defense from the north. Joshua knew that his conquests in Canaan would not be secure without defeating the coalition headed by Jabin, king of Hazor (Josh. 11:1-23). Deborah and Barak also conquered Hazor when its king sought to reestablish Canaanite control in the Jezreel Valley (Judg. 4:1–5:31). Solomon fortified Hazor along with Gezer and

Megiddo in his attempt to control traffic on the International Highway (1 Kings 9:15). In the early days of the divided monarchy, Ben-hadad, king of Damascus, captured the entire Huleh Basin from Israel (1 Kings 15:20), and the region remained a "land between," coveted by both Syria and Israel, throughout the biblical period.

Eventually larger powers—the Assyrians (2 Kings 15:29), Babylonians, Persians, Greeks, Seleucids, Ptolemies, and Romans—seized the Huleh Basin to secure their position in the area. By New Testament times, the Huleh sat in the middle of Jewish and Gentile populations. In offering the wealth and opportunities of the world, this region became a true testing ground of faith.

> From at least the time of Alexander the Great's conquest of Palestine, the area around the springs feeding the eastern-most tributary of the Jordan River was a sanctuary for Pan, the Greco-Roman god of shepherds, hunters, and fertility. This region was called Panias (modern Banyas), in Pan's honor. Herod the Great built a temple here, which he dedicated to Caesar Augustus. Herod Philip made Panias the capital of his realm upon the death of his father, changing its name to Caesarea Philippi. It was in this region, full in the face of the Greco-Roman world, that Jesus challenged His disciples, "Who do you say that I am?" (Matt. 16:15). It was also here that Jesus first mentioned the church (Matt. 16:18).

The Huleh Basin is awash with water and fertility. As the northern gateway into Palestine, its control is critical for anyone who seeks to live securely in the land. Like the coastal plain, this basin witnessed the ebb and flow of foreign powers through the Levant, and it remained a region that challenged the efforts of ancient Israel and Judea to control their own destiny.

THE EASTERN REGIONS
(Transjordan)

The eastern regions of Palestine lie east of the rift valley: Bashan, Gilead, Ammon, the Medeba Plateau, Moab, and Edom. While most of the events of the Bible took place west of the Jordan River, the regions of Transjordan were closely tied to the overall sweep of the biblical story. Except for Bashan, each is located today in the Hashemite Kingdom of Jordan.

Bashan

Bashan is an expansive plateau in northern Transjordan stretching from Mount Hermon to south of the Yarmuk River (Num. 21:33; Deut. 3:1-11; 29:7). During the time of the New Testament, the western portion of Bashan—the slopes facing the Huleh Basin—was

Bashan.

called Gaulanitis. The name Gaulanitis is a latinized form of Golan, the Old Testament city of refuge in the region (Deut. 4:43; Josh. 21:27). Today, most of Gaulanitis falls within the borders of the Golan Heights, a narrow buffer between the modern states of Israel and Syria.

The topography of Bashan is relatively flat but drops dramatically into the Huleh Basin in the west. These rocky slopes provide excellent grazing land for cattle, which were renowned in antiquity for their strength (Ps. 22:12) and fatness (Ezek. 39:18; Amos 4:1). In the flatter areas, the basalt boulders have broken down into a dark, rich soil that was farmed extensively for wheat during the Roman period.

Rainfall on the western portions of Bashan is abundant, up to 40 inches annually. The rain gradually tapers, however, toward the vast eastern desert, as it does in all of Transjordan. Most of the rainfall on Bashan drains into the upper tributaries of the Yarmuk River, which curls around the region on the south and east. The large Yarmuk canyon enters the Jordan River south of the Sea of Galilee. To the north, Mount Hermon receives heavy snow each year; one of its Arabic names, *Jebel eth-Thalj,* means "mountain of the snow."

At 9,233 feet Mount Hermon is by far the highest peak in Palestine. If the wintertime skies are exceptionally clear, snowy Hermon can be seen from the hills northwest of Jerusalem, 115 miles away. The Bible sometimes calls Hermon by its Phoenician name, Sirion, or its Amorite name, Senir (Deut. 3:9; Ps. 29:6). The name Hermon comes from a Hebrew word that means "devoted," aptly conveying the mountain's sacred character in both Canaanite and Israelite religion (cp. Judg. 3:3; 1 Chron. 5:23). Psalm 48:1-2 combines images of Hermon with Mount Zion in speaking of the holy habitation of God (cp. Ps. 68:15-16).

The Bible speaks glowingly of the fertility of Bashan, as it does the Plain of Sharon, Mount Carmel, Lebanon, and Gilead. "I will bring Israel back to his own pasture and he will graze on Carmel and Bashan" (Jer 50:19 NIV), and "Shepherd your people with your staff, the flock of your inheritance, which lives by itself in a forest, in fertile pasturelands. Let them feed in Bashan and Gilead as in days long ago" (Mic. 7:14). More often, however, the prophets spoke of Bashan's withering up as a sure sign of God's judgment (Isa. 33:9; Nah. 1:4; Zech. 11:2).

Politically Bashan has always been a wide open buffer zone between Syria and Israel, connected to them by international highways yet belonging securely to neither. One branch of the International Highway leaving Damascus skirts Mount Hermon on its way to Galilee and the coast. The other branch, the Transjordanian Highway, takes a southern course through the Old Testament cities of Karnaim (Gen. 14:5), Ashtoroth (Gen. 14:5; Josh. 9:10; 12:4; 13:12, 31) and Edrei (Deut. 1:4; 3:1,10), on its way to Ammon, Moab, Edom, and the Arabian Peninsula. These international highways are joined by cross routes bisecting Bashan east to west.

Moses conquered Bashan from the Amorite king Og (Num. 21:33-35; Deut. 3:1-7), giving the region to the tribe of Manasseh (Deut. 3:13; Josh. 13:29-30). During the monarchy, the kings of Israel and Syria fought continuously over Bashan (2 Kings 10:32-33; 14:25). Any time a king of Syria appeared within the borders of Israel or Transjordan (e.g., 1 Kings 20:1-3; 22:1-3; 2 Kings 6:24), it can be assumed that Bashan had been taken first. Overrun by the Assyrians in the late eighth century, Bashan never again was an integral part of ancient Israel. In New Testament times Bashan belonged to the territory of Philip, son of Herod the Great, yet remained largely a Gentile region.

The fertility of Bashan and its position as a buffer between Israel and Syria underlies its strategic role in the biblical story. Here Israel met Syria face to face. Not insignificantly, it was somewhere on Bashan's open expanse that Saul of Tarsus met God visibly and became Christianity's first great missionary to the Gentiles (Acts 9:1-6).

Gilead and Ammon

Three regions, Lower Gilead, the Dome of Gilead, and Ammon, make up the hills of central Transjordan. These lie across the Jordan River from the hill country of Ephraim and Manasseh, the heartland of ancient Israel. The landforms, soils, and water resources of these three regions are quite varied, as were the lifestyle patterns of their inhabitants in antiquity.

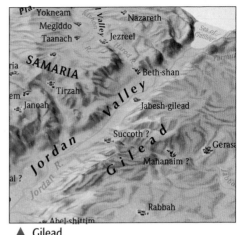

▲ Gilead.

The meaning of the word "Gilead" is unknown. Genesis 31:45-48 connects it to Galeed, "a heap of witness," i.e., a pile of stones placed as a memorial, but this may be simply a pun on the names. Gilead may also be related to a word meaning "strong" or "sturdy," perhaps reflecting the strength of the hills that dominate the region. The Bible's use of Gilead is also indefinite; sometimes the term is limited to the hills around the Jabbok River; other times it seems to refer to the entire region of Transjordan that was under Israelite control (Josh. 22:13; Ps. 60:7).

Lower Gilead is a relatively level plateau south of the Yarmuk River composed of soft Eocene limestone and Senonian chalk. The elevations of Lower Gilead do not exceed 1,650 feet, and rainfall can reach 24 inches annually. The soils of Lower Gilead are not as rich as those of Bashan, but they are more easily plowed and, like Bashan, well suited for grains.

Lower Gilead fell within the southern portion of the kingdom of Og, and after being conquered by Moses, it was allotted to the tribe of Manasseh (Num. 21:33-35; Deut. 3:1-12). Its biblical name during the time of the judges was Havvoth-jair, "the villages of Jair," after Jair, a descendant of Manasseh (Num. 32:40-41; Judg. 10:3-5). The primary cities in Lower Gilead during the Old Testament period were Jabesh-gilead, which figured prominently in the life of King Saul (1 Sam. 11:1-11; 31:11-13; cp. Judg. 21:6-14), and Ramoth-gilead, the key to military strategy in the entire region. Ancient Ramoth-gilead lay at the juncture of the Transjordanian Highway and the primary route running through the Harod and Jezreel Valleys. Ahab lost his life in an attempt to control this strategic crossroads and thereby check Syria's moves toward Israel (1 Kings 22:1-40; cp. 2 Kings

8:28–9:13). During the time of the New Testament, Gadara and Pella, two cities of the Decapolis, dominated the region.

South of Lower Gilead is a rugged, uplifted dome of hard Cenomanian limestone commonly known as the Dome of Gilead. Elevations here reach 4,091 feet, considerably higher than the hills of Ephraim and Manasseh west of the Jordan. The Dome of Gilead has been deeply cut in two by the Jabbok River, a huge open wedge running east-west and joining the Jordan River midway between the Sea of Galilee and the Dead Sea. Because of its elevation, the Dome of Gilead is generally wetter than the hills west of the Jordan, and snowfall on its heights is not uncommon. The terra rosa soil of Gilead supports the traditional hill country crops (grapes, olives, figs, pomegranates, and almonds), allowing the ancient Israelites to feel at home here.

The rugged hill country of Gilead.

After Moses conquered the Amorite kingdom of Sihon and the kingdom of Og in Bashan, he allowed the tribes of Reuben, Gad, and a portion of Manasseh to settle in areas of Transjordan that were not already considered part of the homelands of Ammon, Moab, or Edom (Num. 21:21-35; 32:1-42; 34:13-15; Deut. 2:26–3:17; 29:7-8). Gad settled in the Jordan Valley, on the western slopes of the Lower Gilead and the Dome of Gilead, and at the northern edge of the Medeba Plateau.

The Prophet Jeremiah spoke of balm in Gilead (Jer. 8:22; 46:11) as a metaphor of "medicine" that could cure Israel's sin (cp. Jer. 51:8). Scanty textual evidence suggests that balm is a kind of a spice with medicinal qualities derived from plant resin, although its exact identification is unknown (cp. Gen. 37:25). The value of balm can be seen in Ezekiel 27:17, which notes that Israel exported balm to Tyre, apparently for distribution on Tyre's vast Mediterranean trading network.

Like the remote hills of Upper Galilee, the Dome of Gilead was primarily dotted by farming villages during the Old Testament period. The major cities in the region at the time, Penuel (Gen. 32:30-31; 1 Kings 12:25) and Mahanaim (Gen. 32:2), were located deep in the cleft of the Jabbok, while Succoth (Judg. 8:4-16) guarded the opening of the Jabbok to the Jordan Valley. The main city in the days of the New Testament, Gerasa (modern Jerash, the best-preserved Roman city in the world), belonged to the Decapolis.

Throughout biblical history the Dome of Gilead was a kind of frontier land for Israel, considered part of their homeland but a bit removed from the main line of events. Jacob (Gen. 32:1-32), Gideon (Judg. 8:1-21), and Jephthah (Judg. 10:6–12:7) all met adversaries here, while Ish-bosheth (2 Sam. 2:8), Abner (2 Sam 2:24-29), David (2 Sam. 17:24-29), and Jeroboam (1 Kings 12:25) used the rugged hills of Gilead as a place of refuge. During the time of the New Testament, Herod Antipas, ruler of Galilee, governed Perea ("beyond the Jordan"), the western portion of this region (Matt. 4:25).

A relatively small basin of soft Senonian chalk tucked below the southeastern rim of the Dome of Gilead formed the heartland of the Old Testament kingdom of Ammon (Num. 21:24; Judg. 10:6-7; 11:4-6; 2 Sam. 10:1-19). This region separates the fertile agricultural lands of Gilead from the open desert, and both farmers and shepherds have been able to make a living there. Rainfall begins to taper in Ammon, but a few springs and an upper tributary of the Jabbok that bisects the region insures reasonable supplies of water.

During the Old Testament period the capital city of Ammon was Rabbah (or Rabbah of the Ammonites, Deut. 3:11; Josh. 13:25). During the time of the New Testament, the name of this city, now a member of the Decapolis, was Philadelphia. From here the Transjordanian Highway splits into two branches. One of these, the King's Highway, drops south to connect Ammon with the ancient capitals of Moab and Edom (Num. 20:17). The other, the "Way of the Wilderness of Moab," bypasses the Arnon and Zered river canyons along the edge of the desert to the east (Deut. 2:8). Today, the Ammon basin is filled to overflowing with the city of Amman, the capital of the Hashemite Kingdom of Jordan, while Jordan's main north-south highway follows the line of the eastern branch of the Transjordanian Highway, now called the "Desert Highway."

Ezekiel's oracle against the Ammonites speaks of Ammon's tenuous position between the land of the farmer and the land of the shepherd: "Therefore I am going to give you to the people of the East as a possession. They will set up their camps and pitch their tents among you; they will eat your fruit and drink your milk. I will turn

Rabbah into a pasture for camels and Ammon into a resting place for sheep. Then you will know that I am the LORD" (Ezek. 25:4-5 NIV).

Israel was attracted to the hills directly east of the Jordan River but found them to be a frontier that was hard to control. The rugged Jabbok canyon served as a place of refuge and escape for Israelites who lived west of the Jordan. The cities of the Decapolis secured Rome's eastern frontier in Transjordan during the time of the New Testament.

Moab and the Medeba Plateau

The heartland of ancient Moab was the high, hilly region lying between the Arnon and Zered river canyons east of the southern half of the Dead Sea, approximately 30 x 30 miles in size. This is a mixed region of Cenomanian limestone and Senonian chalk, with large outcrop-

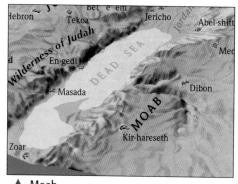

▲ Moab.

pings of basalt on the higher elevations. The highest hills in Moab run about 3,600 feet, but an elevation of 4,282 feet is reached in the south above the Zered.

North of the Arnon is a lower plateau of Senonian chalk (approximately 2,300 feet in elevation) that the Bible calls the *mishor* ("plateau" or "tableland," Deut. 3:10; Josh. 13:9,16). Cenomanian limestone and reddish Nubian sandstone are exposed on the western scarp of this plateau as it drops into the rift valley and Dead Sea. A common name for this region is the Medeba Plateau, after Medeba (modern Madaba), its most important city today.

The remains of a mosaic floor from the ruins of a sixth century A.D. Byzantine church in the city of Madaba depict the oldest known map of Palestine. This beautiful map was originally 77 x 20 feet in size and showed the world of the eastern Mediterranean from Lebanon to the Nile Delta. Unfortunately, only the area from south central Palestine to the Nile, about one third of the original remains. The Medeba map is an invaluable primary source for the geography and settlement of the land of Palestine during the Byzantine period. Of particular note is the map's depiction of Jerusalem, which graphically shows the primary streets, gates, and buildings of the city of that time.

The Arnon (Deut. 2:24) and Zered (Deut. 2:13), like the Yarmuk and Jabbok further north, are huge water erosion canyons that have cut deeply into the Transjordanian hills, channeling most of the region's rainfall into the rift valley. At 2,300 feet deep, the Arnon is perhaps the most dramatic of all. From rim to rim the Arnon spans over three miles, and the torturous road that crosses this chasm today, close to the ancient route of the King's Highway, can take one to two hours to traverse by bus.

While rainfall on the Dead Sea scarcely tops four inches per year, these higher hills to the east receive amounts only somewhat less than the hills west of the Jordan—on average 10 inches on the Medeba Plateau and 16 in Moab proper. During the biblical period, this was the land of the shepherd Mesha, king of Moab and contemporary of Ahab, where he "raised sheep, and he had to supply the king of Israel with a hundred thousand lambs and with the wool of a hundred thousand rams" (2 Kings 3:4 NIV). Today, the level chalk tableland north of the Arnon is one of Jordan's prime grain producing areas.

The tranquil book of Ruth is set in the turbulent period of the judges. The story opens with a famine gripping Bethlehem (Ruth 1:1), a not-too-unusual occurrence for a city whose agricultural lands drop toward the chalk wilderness east of the watershed ridge. Naomi, her husband Elimelech, and their two sons left their ancestral home in Bethlehem to journey to the higher hills of Moab to the east (Ruth 1:2), an area where rainfall was more reliable, if less in overall amounts. Here they tried to piece together an agricultural and shepherding existence like the one they left behind in Judah. Naomi eventually returned home to Bethlehem with only her daughter-in-law Ruth (Ruth 1:6-19).

During the Old Testament period, the major cities on the Medeba Plateau and in Moab were located on the route of the King's Highway. From north to south, these were Heshbon (Num. 21:25-26), Medeba (Num. 21:30) and Dibon (Num. 21:30) north of the Arnon, and Ar (Num. 21:28) and Kir-hareseth (2 Kings 3:25) in Moab proper. Heshbon was the city of Sihon, whose Amorite kingdom Moses and the Israelites conquered on their way to Canaan (Num. 21:21-31; Deut. 2:24-37). Kir-hareseth was the capital of the kingdom of Moab; the remains of the Crusader castle of Kerak dominate the site today.

Of note during the time of the New Testament is Machaerus, Herod the Great's desert fortress east of the rift valley. Machaerus sits on the scarp of the Medeba Plateau east of the Dead Sea. According to Josephus, John the Baptist was beheaded here by Herod Antipas, who ruled the region of Perea which included Machaerus, at the behest of his new wife, Herodias (Mark 6:14-29).

Throughout the biblical period, the Medeba Plateau was a frontier zone between the kingdoms of Moab and Israel, and each tried to contain the other by seizing the plateau and its highways. Moses gave the Medeba Plateau to the tribe of Reuben after conquering Sihon (Josh. 13:15-23), but by the time of the judges, the Moabite king Eglon had crossed both the plateau and the Jordan River to set up residence in Jericho, the city of palms (Judg. 3:12-30). Later, Moab and, by implication, the Medeba Plateau were subject to both David (2 Sam. 8:2,11-12) and Ahab, king of Israel (2 Kings 1:1). Ahab's claim on the plateau had been anticipated when Hiel of Bethel rebuilt Jericho (1 Kings 16:34), securing that city as a launching pad for Israelite control east of the Jordan. After Ahab's death, Mesha king of Moab pushed Moabite influence back onto the Medeba Plateau (2 Kings 3:4-5); the Mesha Stele (Moabite Stone) tells of this expansion from Moab's point of view. Moab remained Israel's eastern nemesis throughout the period of the monarchy and was the object of prophetic wrath by Amos (2:1-3), Isaiah (15:1–16:14), and Jeremiah (48:1-47).

View of the Jordan Valley from the top of Mount Nebo looking toward Jericho.

According to Deuteronomy 34:1-3, Moses viewed the Canaan from Mount Nebo, the top of Pisgah, northeast of the Dead Sea. It is unclear from the biblical texts whether Mount Nebo is a range of hills of which Pisgah is a single peak or vice versa (Num. 21:20; 23:14; Deut. 3:27; 32:49; 34:1). While there is a traditional site of Mount Nebo today, complete with Byzantine church and beautiful mosaics, it is impossible to know which mountain of many in the area Moses actually climbed. The traditional spot provides a breathtaking panorama of Canaan, including spires of the Mount of Olives on a clear day, but it is geographically impossible to see everything that Moses saw from this location without "spiritual eyes."

Like Bashan, the Medeba Plateau was an important "land between" in the biblical story. Here, on its open expanse, Israel met Moab face to face. Each struggled to control the plateau as they sought to secure their position in the hills east of the Jordan River.

Edom

Stretching 110 miles from the Zered canyon to the Gulf of Aqaba, Edom is the largest region of Transjordan. The geography of Edom is complex, with limestone plateaus in the north giving way to a rugged and awesome sandstone topography in the south. Most of Edom is true desert. Here the open expanse of the vast Arabian Peninsula

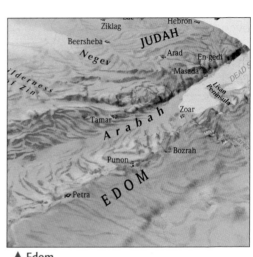

▲ Edom.

encroaches closely onto the settled lands of Palestine.

The word "Edom" is derived from a Hebrew word that means "red," probably reflecting the reddish color of the sandstone cliffs in the region that front the rift valley. Edom is an alternate name for Esau, the brother of Jacob (Israel) and ancestor of the Edomites (Gen. 25:30; 36:19). The name "Esau" is related to Seir, yet another name for Edom (Gen. 14:6; 36:19-20; Deut. 1:2; Josh. 24:4). Both Esau and Seir apparently come from a Hebrew word meaning "hairy." It has

▲ Gulf of Eilat/Gulf of Aqaba.

been suggested that the trees that lined the scarp of Edom in antiquity looked "hairy" when viewed from the rift valley below, and hence the name, but this is unlikely.

The narrow gulf of the Red Sea that touches the southern point of Palestine is called the Gulf of Eilat today by Israelis and the Gulf of Aqaba by Jordanians. The former name is more appropriate when discussing the Negev, while the latter is best used in the context of Edom (cp. 1 Kings 9:26)

Geologically, the land of Edom can be divided into three sub-regions:

• The northernmost sub-region, from the Zered to the vicinity of the city of Punion 25 miles south, was the heartland of the Old Testament Kingdom of Edom. Elevations reach 5,384 feet, and rainfall averages around 14 inches on the heights overlooking the arid rift below. Limited agriculture is possible along this narrow north-south band, but just to the east the climate of the vast eastern desert overwhelms the land.

• The central sub-region is composed of a high limestone plateau that stretches for 50 miles south of Punion. The highest point, near Petra, reaches 5,696 feet. Rainfall averages 6–10 inches along the western scarp, and because of its height—which is significantly greater than the hills of the Negev west of the rift—snow is not unusual during the winter. Mountains of red sandstone line the rift valley, and the view through them into the rift from Petra is truly astonishing.

• The central plateau ends abruptly with a dramatic scarp running perpendicular to the rift valley. Below lies a vast expanse of rugged sandstone and granite peaks, a complex maze of sails jutting out of a vast sea of sand. Spectacular vistas are found in the Wadi Rum, the southeastern portion of this sub-region. To the southwest, thick bands of copper and iron lace the surface of the hills. Rainfall here averages less than two inches per year. Geologically and culturally, this is the land of Arabia.

The primary cities of Edom during the Old Testament period were the oasis of Bozrah (Gen. 36:33; Isa. 34:6; Amos 1:11-12) and Sela (2 Kings 14:7; Isa. 16:1), both located in the northern sub-region. The magnificent remains of the rose-red city of Petra, capital of the vast Nabatean trading network during the New Testament period, are tucked away in the sandstone hills along the western scarp of the central sub-region.

The mountainous landscape of the land of Edom.

Both Sela (Hebrew) and Petra (Greek) mean "rock," and both are apt names for cities in the bare, rugged hills of Edom. Because of the similarity of name, it is often thought that Old Testament Sela was located at what was to become Petra.

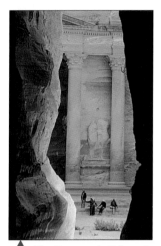

▲ The Treasury building of ancient Petra as seen from the only entranceway into the city.

It is more likely, however, that Sela was further north, in the vicinity of Bozrah, the heartland of the Edomite kingdom.

The King's Highway, linking Bozrah and Sela to the capitals of Moab and Ammon, joins its eastern branch, the Desert Highway, just above the scarp that drops into Edom's southern sub-region. To the south, this international route connects Transjordan to the Red Sea and the great spice route of Arabia. An important side route links Bozrah to the Negev, funneling international traffic from Edom to Egypt and the Mediterranean.

Unconquered by Moses (Deut. 2:1-7), the Edomites remained the nemesis of Israel and Judah throughout the monarchy. Edom's natural point of expansion was to the west, into the Negev, which brought its people into direct conflict with Judah, who was seeking to expand into the same region (2 Sam. 8:14; 1 Kings 22:47-49; 2 Kings 8:20-22; 14:7; 16:5-6; 2 Chron. 20:1-37). Both wanted to control the lucrative trade flowing out of Arabia and Egypt, and each tried to establish a port on the Gulf of Eilat. When Judah fell to the Babylonians—apparently with Edomite assistance—the Edomites were finally able to pour unchecked into the Negev; this fueled some of the prophetic utterances of Jeremiah (49:7-22) and Obadiah (1-21). By the time of the New Testament, a remnant of the Edomites, now known by their Greek name, Idumeans, had settled in the Judean shephelah. Edom proper—and most of the Negev—came under the control of the powerful trading empire of the Nabateans.

Although the Nabateans are not mentioned in the New Testament, twice persons associated with the Nabateans are. The first century historian Josephus mentions that the woman Herod Antipas divorced in order to marry Herodias, the wife of his brother Philip, was a Nabatean queen, the daughter of Aretas (cp. Mark 6:17-29; Josephus Ant. xviii.5.2). The Apostle Paul writes that when he was in Damascus, the city governor under King Aretas tried to arrest him, but he slipped out of the city by being lowered from a window in the wall in a basket (2 Cor. 11:30-33). In both cases, the Aretas in question was probably Aretas IV, the greatest builder of Petra.

High and majestic, the mountains of Edom tower over the rift valley and Negev. From its secure heights, the Edomites, ancestral brothers of Israel, challenged Judah's claim to the southern approaches of Palestine.

MAPS OF BIBLE LANDS

15▸ THE TABLE OF NATIONS

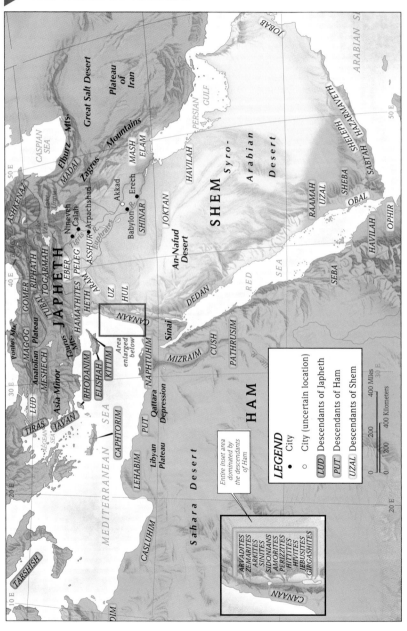

Genesis 10:1
This is the account of Shem, Ham, and Japheth, Noah's sons, who themselves had sons after the flood.

16 ▶ THE MIGRATION OF ABRAHAM

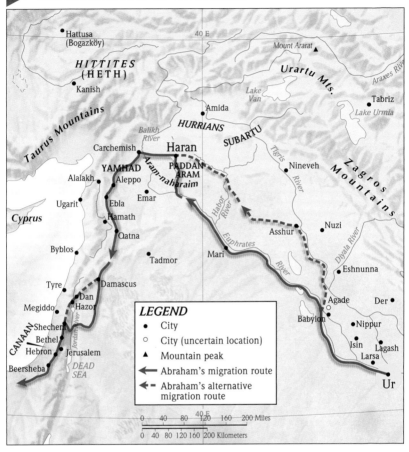

Genesis 11:31

Terah took his son Abram, his grandson Lot son of Haran, and his daughter-in-law Sarai, the wife of his son Abram, and together they set out from Ur of the Chaldeans to go to Canaan. But when they came to Haran, they settled there.

Genesis 12:1,4

The LORD had said to Abram, "Leave your country, your people and your father's household, and go to the land I will show you.

So Abram left, as the LORD had told him; and Lot went with him. Abram was seventy-five years old when he set out from Haran.

17 ABRAHAM IN CANAAN

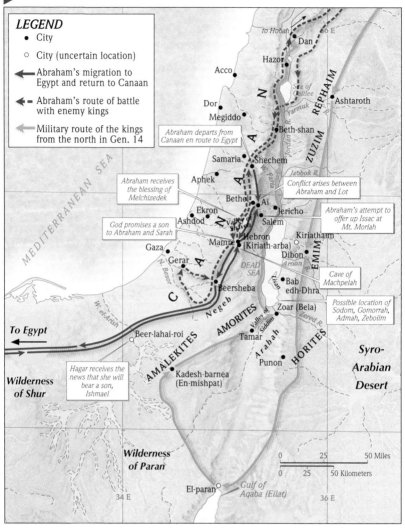

LEGEND
- City
- City (uncertain location)
- Abraham's migration to Egypt and return to Canaan
- Abraham's route of battle with enemy kings
- Military route of the kings from the north in Gen. 14

Genesis 12:10
Now there was a famine in the land, and Abram went down to Egypt to live there for a while because the famine was severe.

18 ▶ TRAVELS OF JACOB

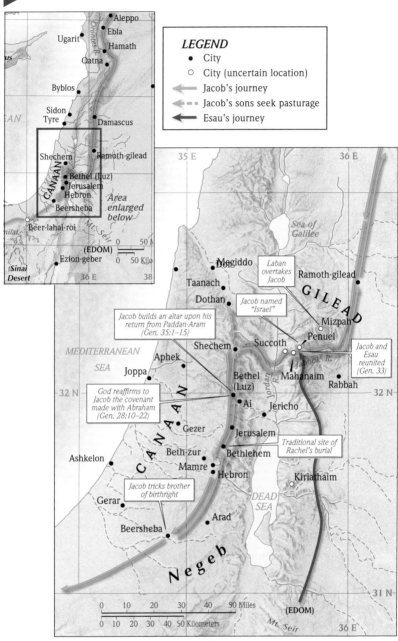

LEGEND
- ● City
- ○ City (uncertain location)
- ← Jacob's journey
- ◀= = = Jacob's sons seek pasturage
- ◀ Esau's journey

Laban overtakes Jacob

Jacob named "Israel"

Jacob builds an altar upon his return from Paddan-Aram (Gen. 35:1–15)

Jacob and Esau reunited (Gen. 33)

God reaffirms to Jacob the covenant made with Abraham (Gen. 28:10–22)

Traditional site of Rachel's burial

Jacob tricks brother of birthright

Genesis 28:12-13

He had a dream in which he saw a stairway resting on the earth, with its top reaching to heaven., and the angels of God were ascending and descending on it.

There above it stood the LORD, and he said, "I am the LORD, the God of your father Abraham and the God of Isaac. I will give you and your descendents the land on which you are lying."

19 ▶ THE JOURNEYS OF JOSEPH

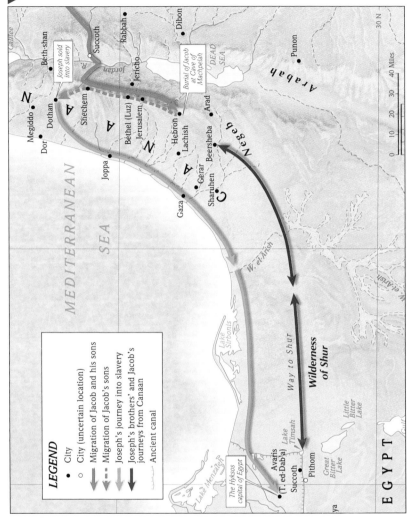

Genesis 37:3-4

Now Israel loved Joseph more than any of his other sons, because he had been born to him in his old age; and he made a richly ornamented robe for him. When his brothers saw that their father loved him more than any of them, they hated him and could not speak a kind word to him.

Genesis 46:2-4

And God spoke to Israel in a vision at night and said, "Jacob! Jacob!" "Here I am," he replied.

"I am God, the God of your father," he said. "Do not be afraid to go down to Egypt, for I make you into a great nation there. I will go down to Egypt with you, and I will surely bring you back again. And Joseph's own hand will close your eyes."

20 ▶ THE ROUTE OF THE EXODUS

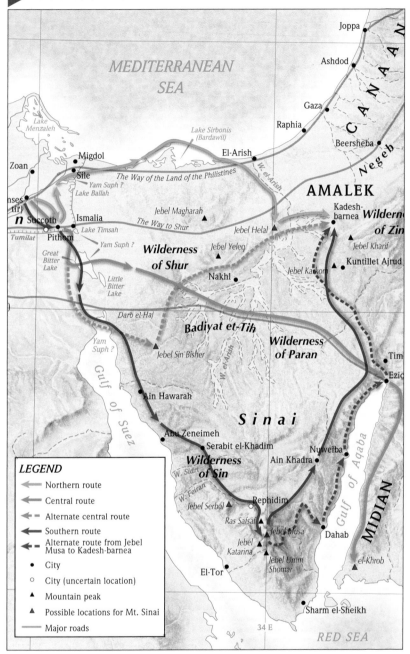

Exodus 14:21-22

Then Moses stretched out his hand over the sea, and all that night the LORD drove the sea back with a strong east wind and turned it into dry land. The waters were divided, and the Israelites went through the sea on dry ground, with a wall of water on their right hand and on their left.

21 ▶ JOURNEY OF THE SPIES

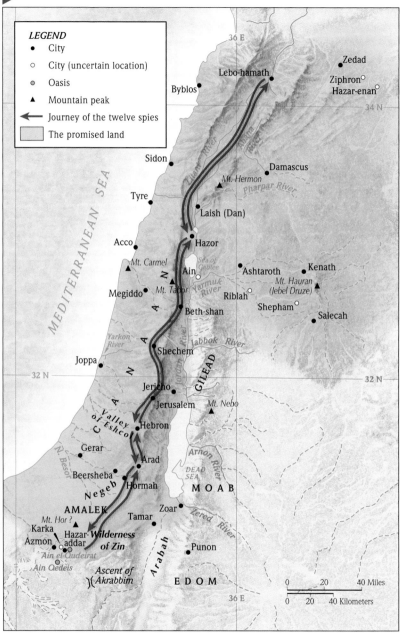

Numbers 13:1-2,32

The Lord said to Moses, "Send some men to explore the land of Canaan, which I am giving to the Israelites. From each ancestral tribe send one of its leaders."

And they spread among the Israelites a bad report about the land they had explored. They said, "The land we explored devours those living in it. All the people we saw there are of great size.

22 ▶ KADESH BARNEA

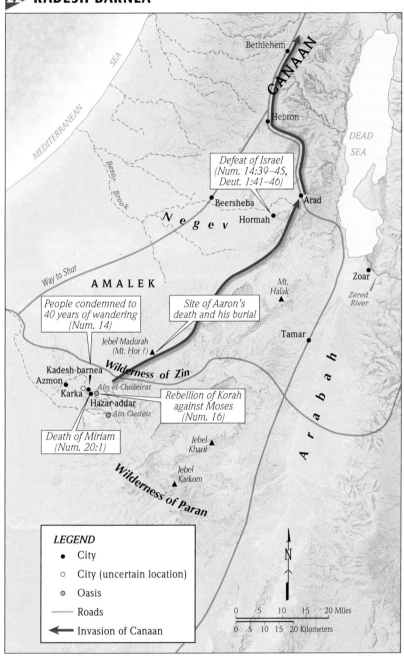

Numbers 14:2

Take a census of the whole Israelite community by their clans and families, listing every man by name, one by one.

23▶ THE JOURNEY FROM KADESH BARNEA TO THE PLAINS OF MOAB

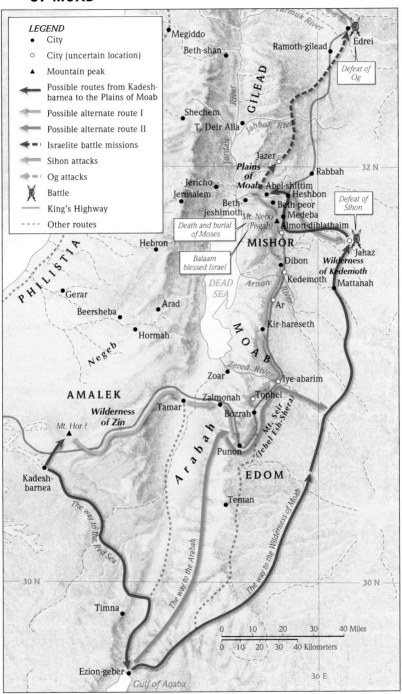

Deuteronomy 2 :2-3
Then the LORD said to me, "You have made your way around this hill country long enough; now turn north."

24▶ JOSHUA'S CENTRAL AND SOUTHERN CAMPAIGNS

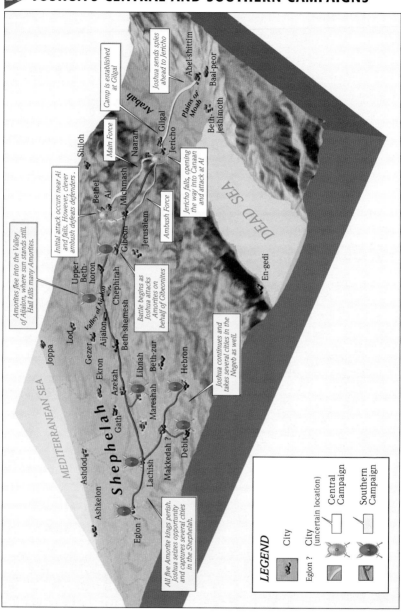

Joshua 10:12-13

On the day the Lord gave the Amorites over to Israel, Joshua said to the Lord in the presence of Israel:

"O sun, stand still over Gibeon, O moon, over the Valley of Aijalon."

So the sun stood still, and the moon stopped, till the nation avenged itself on its enemies, as it is written in the Book of Jashar. The sun stopped in the middle of the sky, and delayed going down about a full day.

25 JOSHUA'S NORTHERN CAMPAIGN

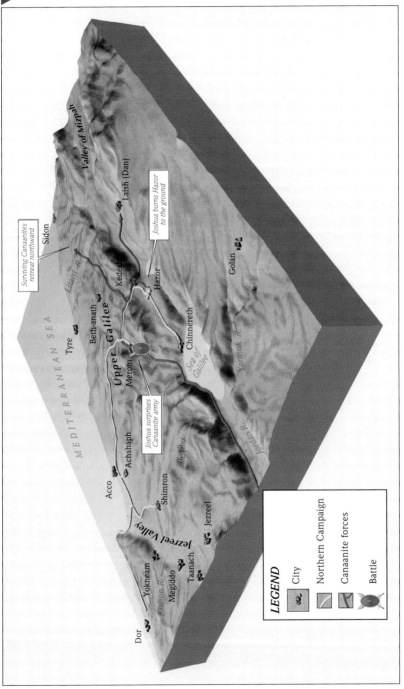

Joshua 11:10
At that time Joshua turned back and captured Hazor and put its king to the sword. (Hazor had been the head of all these kingdoms.)

26 LIMITS OF ISRAELITE SETTLEMENT AND THE LAND TO BE CONQUERED

LEGEND
- • City
- ○ City (uncertain location)
- ◉ City specified by Judges 1 as not taken by Israel
- ▲ Mountain peak
- Limit of Israelite control
- Areas yet to be conquered

Amorites pressure tribe of Dan near Aijalon (Judg. 1:34–36)

Joshua 13:1

When Joshua was old and well advanced in years, the LORD said to him, "You are very old, and there are still very large areas of land to be taken over.

27 THE TRIBAL ALLOTMENTS OF ISRAEL

LEGEND
- City
- ○ City (uncertain location)
- ▲ Mountain peak

Joshua 19:49-50

When they had finished dividing the land into its allotted portions, the Israelites gave Joshua son of Nun an inheritance among them, as the LORD commanded. They gave him the town he asked for—Timnath Serah in the hill country of Ephraim. And he built up the town and settled there.

28▶ LEVITICAL CITIES AND CITIES OF REFUGE

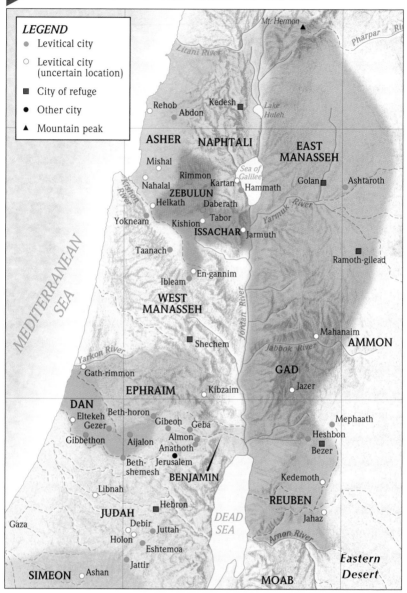

LEGEND
- ● Levitical city
- ○ Levitical city (uncertain location)
- ■ City of refuge
- ● Other city
- ▲ Mountain peak

Joshua 21:8
So the Israelites allotted to the Levites these towns and their pasturelands, as the LORD had commanded through Moses.

Joshua 20:1-3
Then the LORD said to Joshua: "Tell the Israelites to designate the cities of refuge, as I instructed you through Moses, so that anyone who kills a person accidentally and unintentionally may flee there and find protection from the avenger of blood."

29 THE JUDGES OF ISRAEL

LEGEND

GIDEON Major judges

TOLA Other judges

• City

○ City (uncertain location)

▲ Mountain peak

SHAMGAR (Judges 3: 31)

ELON (Judges 12:11–12)

GIDEON (Judges 6:1–8:27)

TOLA (Judges 10:1–2)

JAIR (Judges 10:3–5)

ABDON (Judges 12:13–15)

JEPHTHAH (Judges 10:6–12:7)

DEBORAH (Judges 4:1–5:31)

EHUD (Judges 3:12–30)

SAMSON (Judges 13:1–16:31)

IBZAN (Judges 12:8–10)

OTHNIEL (Judges 3:7–11)

Mt. Hermon

Pharpar

Ijon

Tyre

Dan (Laish)

Beth-anath

Kedesh

Lake Huleh

Achzib

Hazor

Acco

ASHER

NAPHTALI

EAST MANASSEH

Golan

Ashtaroth

Mt. Carmel

Kishon River

Rimmon

Sea of Galilee

ZEBULUN

Kedesh-naphtali

Yarmuk River

Dor

Megiddo

Mt. Tabor

ISSACHAR

Ophrah

Kamon

Ramoth-gilead

Mt. Gilboa

Beth-shan

WEST MANASSEH

Shamir

Tirzah

Mt. Ebal

Shechem

Zaphon

Succoth

Jordan River

Jabbok River

Pirathon

Mt. Gerizim

Arumah

Adam

GAD

AMMON

Yarkon River

EPHRAIM

Shiloh

Jazer

Upper Beth-horon

Bethel

Mizpah

Gilgal

Rabbah (Amman)

DAN

Lower Beth-horon

Gibeon

Michmash

Jericho

Heshbon

Gezer

Ramah

Bezer

Timnah

Kiriath-jearim

Gibeah

Ekron

Eshtaol

Jerusalem

Mt. Nebo

Ashdod

Zorah

BENJAMIN

Gath

Bethlehem

REUBEN

DEAD SEA

Hebron

Dibon

JUDAH

Debir

Arnon River

Ziklag

SIMEON

Arad

Beersheba

Litani River

SHAMGAR

Judges 21:25

In those days Israel had no king; everyone did as he saw fit.

30 EHUD AND THE OPPRESSION OF THE MOABITES

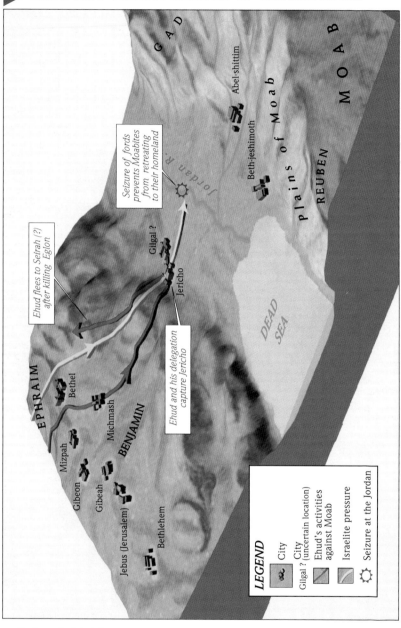

Seizure of fords prevents Moabites from retreating to their homeland

Ehud flees to Seirah (?) after killing Eglon

Ehud and his delegation capture Jericho

Gilgal ?

Jericho

Jordan R.

Abel-shittim

Beth-jeshimoth

Plains of Moab

G A D

M O A B

REUBEN

DEAD SEA

EPHRAIM

Bethel

Mizpah

Michmash

Gibeon

Gibeah

BENJAMIN

Jebus (Jerusalem)

Bethlehem

LEGEND

City

Gilgal ? City (uncertain location)

Ehud's activities against Moab

Israelite pressure

Seizure at the Jordan

Judges 3:14-16

The Israelites were subject to Eglon king of Moab for eighteen years.

Again the Israelites cried out to the LORD, and he gave them a deliverer—Ehud, a left-handed man, the son of Gera the Benjaminite. The Israelites sent him with tribute to Eglon king of Moab. Now Ehud had made a double-edged sword about a foot and a half long, which he strapped to his right thigh under his clothing.

31 ▶ DEBORAH'S VICTORY OVER THE CANAANITES

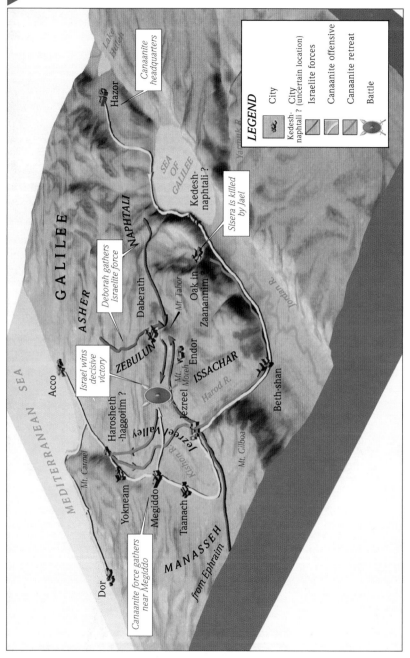

LEGEND

City	
Kedesh-naphtali ?	City (uncertain location)
	Israelite forces
	Canaanite offensive
	Canaanite retreat
	Battle

Canaanite headquarters

Hazor

Lake Huleh

SEA OF GALILEE

Kedesh-naphtali ?

Sisera is killed by Jael

Yarmuk R.

Jordan R.

GALILEE

NAPHTALI

ASHER

Deborah gathers Israelite force

Daberath

Mt. Tabor

Oak in Zaanannim

ZEBULUN

Israel wins decisive victory

Mt. Moreh

Endor

ISSACHAR

Acco

Jezreel

Harod R.

Beth-shan

MEDITERRANEAN SEA

Harosheth-haggoyim ?

Jezreel Valley

Kishon R.

Mt. Gilboa

Mt. Carmel

Yokneam

Megiddo

Taanach

Canaanite force gathers near Megiddo

Dor

MANASSEH

from Ephraim

Judges 4:8-9

Barak said to her, "If you go with me, I will go; but if you don't go with me, I won't go." "Very well," Deborah said, "I will go with you. But because of the way you are going about this, the honor will not be yours, for the LORD will hand Sisera over to a woman." So Deborah went with Barak to Kedesh.

32 GIDEON'S BATTLES WITH THE AMALEKITES

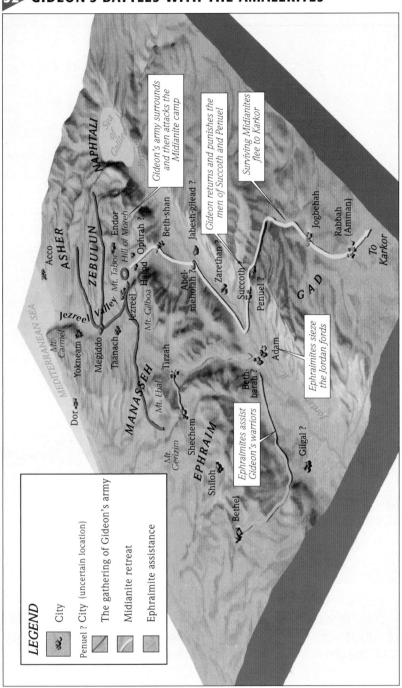

Gideon's army surrounds and then attacks the Midianite camp

Gideon returns and punishes the men of Succoth and Penuel

Surviving Midianites flee to Karkor

Ephraimites sieze the Jordan fords

Ephraimites assist Gideon's warriors

LEGEND

🏠 City

Penuel ? City (uncertain location)

The gathering of Gideon's army

Midianite retreat

Ephraimite assistance

Judges 8:28

Thus Midian was subdued before the Israelites and did not raise its head again. During Gideon's lifetime, the land enjoyed peace forty years.

33 ▶ JEPHTHAH AND THE AMMONITES

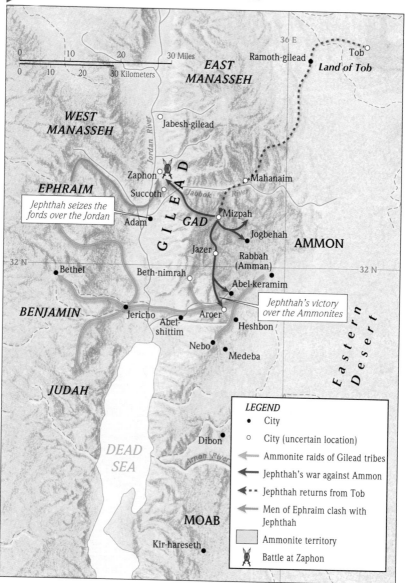

Judges 11:4-6

Some time later, when the Ammonites made war on Israel, the elders of Gilead went to get Jephthah from the land of Tob. "Come," they said, "be our commander, so we can fight the Ammonites."

34 ▶ SAMSON AND THE PHILISTINES

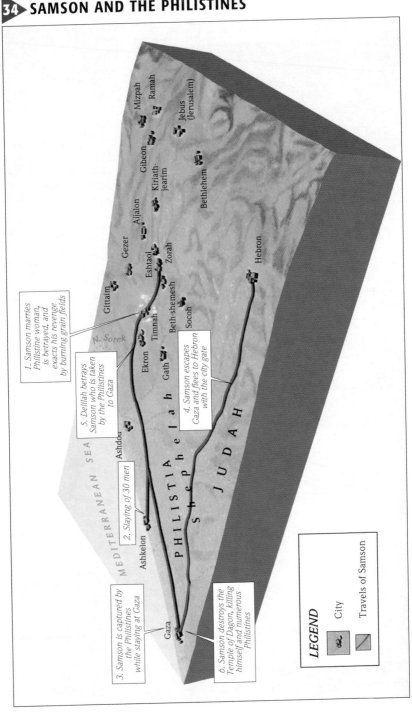

1. Samson marries Philistine woman, is betrayed, and exacts his revenge by burning grain fields

2. Slaying of 30 men

3. Samson is captured by the Philistines while staying at Gaza

4. Samson escapes Gaza and flees to Hebron with the city gate

5. Delilah betrays Samson who is taken by the Philistines to Gaza

6. Samson destroys the Temple of Dagon, killing himself and numerous Philistines

LEGEND
- City
- Travels of Samson

Judges 16:23

Now the rulers of the Philistines assembled to offer a great sacrifice to Dagon their god and to celebrate, saying, "Our god has delivered Samson, our enemy, into our hands."

35 THE BATTLE AT EBENEZER

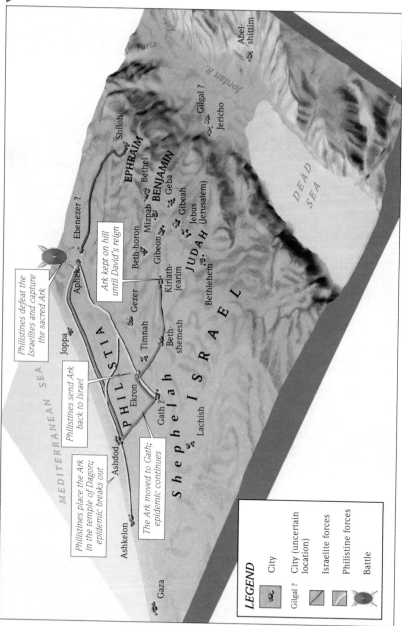

Abel-shittim

Jordan R.

Gilgal ?

Jericho

Shiloh

EPHRAIM

Bethel

BENJAMIN

Ebenezer ?

Mizpah

Beth-horon

Geba

Gibeah

DEAD SEA

Gibeon

Jebus (Jerusalem)

Philistines defeat the Israelites and capture the sacred Ark

Aphek

Ark kept on hill until David's reign

Kiriath-jearim

JUDAH

Joppa

Gezer

Bethlehem

P H I L I S T I A

Timnah

Beth-shemesh

I S R A E L

Philistines send Ark back to Israel

Ekron

S h e p h e l a h

Gath ?

M E D I T E R R A N E A N   S E A

Philistines place the Ark in the temple of Dagon; epidemic breaks out

Ashdod

The Ark moved to Gath; epidemic continues

Lachish

Ashkelon

Gaza

LEGEND

🏛️	City
Gilgal ?	City (uncertain location)
▨	Israelite forces
▨	Philistine forces
⊗	Battle

1 Samuel 4:2-3

The Philistines deployed their forces to meet Israel, and as the battle spread, Israel was defeated by the Philistines, who killed about four thousand of them on the battlefield. When the soldiers returned to camp, the elders of Israel asked, "Why did the LORD bring defeat upon us today before the Philistines? Let us bring the ark of the LORD 's covenant from Shiloh, so that it may go with us and save us from the hand of our enemies."

36 MINISTRY OF SAMUEL AND ANOINTING OF SAUL

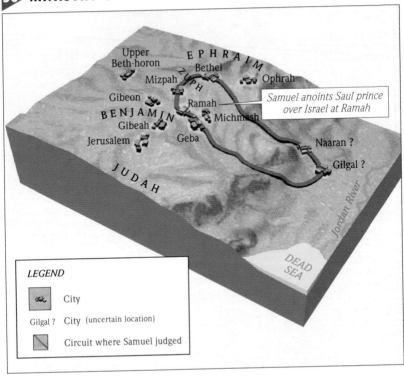

Samuel anoints Saul prince over Israel at Ramah

LEGEND

City

Gilgal ? City (uncertain location)

Circuit where Samuel judged

1 Samuel 7:15-17

Samuel continued as judge over Israel all the days of his life. From year to year he went on a circuit from Bethel to Gilgal to Mizpah, judging Israel in all those places. But he always went back to Ramah, where his home was, and there he also judged Israel. And he built an altar there to the LORD.

 Tel Rama (Ramah)–birthplace of Samuel the prophet.

37 ▶ THE KINGDOM OF SAUL AND HIS WARS

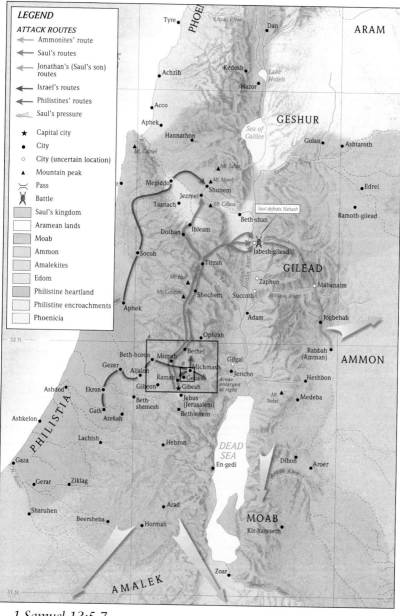

LEGEND

ATTACK ROUTES
- ← Ammonites' route
- ← Saul's routes
- ← Jonathan's (Saul's son) routes
- ← Israel's routes
- ← Philistines' routes
- ← Saul's pressure

- ★ Capital city
- ● City
- ○ City (uncertain location)
- ▲ Mountain peak
- ✕ Pass
- ✕ Battle
- Saul's kingdom
- Aramean lands
- Moab
- Ammon
- Amalekites
- Edom
- Philistine heartland
- Philistine encroachments
- Phoenicia

Saul defeats Nahash

1 Samuel 13:5-7

The Philistines assembled to fight Israel, with three thousand chariots, six thousand charioteers, and soldiers as numerous as the sand on the seashore. They went up and camped at Micmash, east of Beth Aven. When the men of Israel saw that their situation was critical and that their army was hard pressed, they hid in caves and thickets, among the rocks, and in pits and cisterns. Some Hebrews even crossed the Jordan to the land of Gad and Gilead. Saul remained at Gilgal, and all the troops with him were quaking with fear.

38 ▶ DAVID'S FLIGHT FROM SAUL

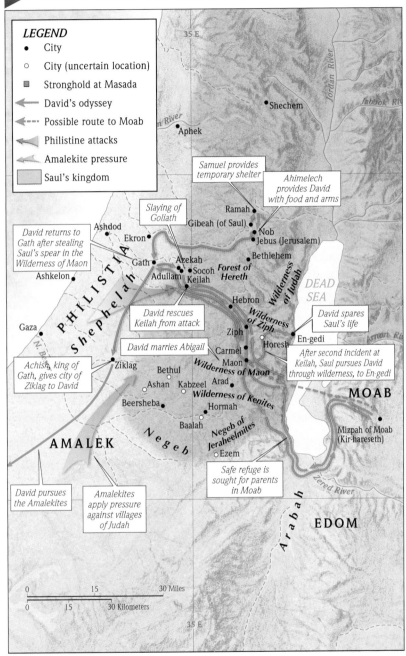

LEGEND
- • City
- ○ City (uncertain location)
- ■ Stronghold at Masada
- ◀— David's odyssey
- ◀--- Possible route to Moab
- ◀ Philistine attacks
- ◀ Amalekite pressure
- Saul's kingdom

Samuel provides temporary shelter

Ahimelech provides David with food and arms

Slaying of Goliath

David returns to Gath after stealing Saul's spear in the Wilderness of Maon

David rescues Keilah from attack

David marries Abigail

David spares Saul's life

Achish, king of Gath, gives city of Ziklag to David

After second incident at Keilah, Saul pursues David through wilderness, to En-gedi

David pursues the Amalekites

Amalekites apply pressure against villages of Judah

Safe refuge is sought for parents in Moab

1 Samuel 24:1-2

After Saul returned from pursuing the Philistines, he was told, "David is in the Desert of En Gedi." So Saul took three thousand chosen men from all Israel and set out to look for David and his men near the Crags of the Wild Goats.

39▶ DAVID'S RISE TO POWER

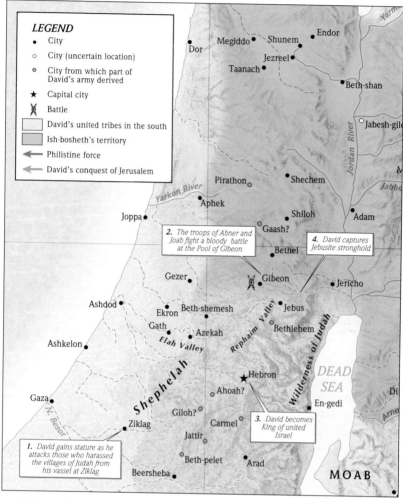

LEGEND
- • City
- ○ City (uncertain location)
- ◉ City from which part of David's army derived
- ★ Capital city
- ✖ Battle
- David's united tribes in the south
- Ish-bosheth's territory
- ← Philistine force
- ← David's conquest of Jerusalem

2. The troops of Abner and Joab fight a bloody battle at the Pool of Gibeon

4. David captures Jebusite stronghold

3. David becomes King of united Israel

1. David gains stature as he attacks those who harassed the villages of Judah from his vassal at Ziklag

2 Samuel 5:6-10

The king and his men marched to Jerusalem to attack the Jebusites, who lived there. The Jebusites said to David, "You will not get in here; even the blind and the lame can ward you off." They thought, "David cannot get in here." Nevertheless, David captured the fortress of Zion, the City of David.

On that day, David said, "Anyone who conquers the Jebusites will have to use the water shaft to reach those 'lame and blind' who are David's enemies." That is why they say, "The 'blind and lame' will not enter the palace."

David then took up residence in the fortress and called it the City of David. He built up the area around it, from the supporting terraces inward. And he became more and more powerful, because the LORD God Almighty was with him.

40 ▶ DAVID'S WARS OF CONQUEST

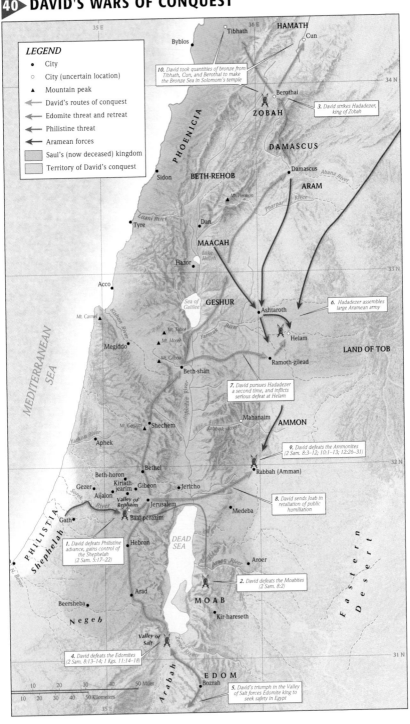

LEGEND
- City
- ○ City (uncertain location)
- ▲ Mountain peak
- ← David's routes of conquest
- ← Edomite threat and retreat
- ← Philistine threat
- ← Aramean forces
- Saul's (now deceased) kingdom
- Territory of David's conquest

10. David took quantities of bronze from Tibhath, Cun, and Berothai to make the Bronze Sea in Solomon's temple

3. David strikes Hadadezer, king of Zobah

6. Hadadezer assembles large Aramean army

7. David pursues Hadadezer a second time, and inflicts serious defeat at Helam

9. David defeats the Ammonites (2 Sam. 8:3–12; 10:1–13; 12:26–31)

8. David sends Joab in retaliation of public humiliation

1. David defeats Philistine advance, gains control of the Shephelah (2 Sam. 5:17–22)

2. David defeats the Moabites (2 Sam. 8:2)

4. David defeats the Edomites (2 Sam. 8:13–14; 1 Kgs. 11:14–18)

5. David's triumph in the Valley of Salt forces Edomite king to seek safety in Egypt

1 Chronicles 18:13
He put garrisons in Edom, and all the Edomites became subject to David. The LORD gave David victory everywhere he went.

41 ▶ KINGDOM OF DAVID AND SOLOMON

1 Kings 2:12
So Solomon sat on the throne of his father David, and his rule was firmly established.

42 SOLOMON'S ECONOMIC ENTERPRISES

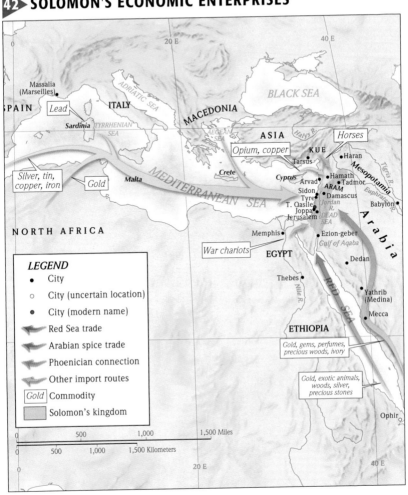

1 Kings 5:10-11

In this way Hiram kept Solomon supplied with all the cedar and pine logs he wanted, and Solomon gave Hiram twenty thousand cors of wheat as food for his household, in addition to twenty thousand baths of pressed olive oil.

43 SOLOMON'S BUILDING ACTIVITIES

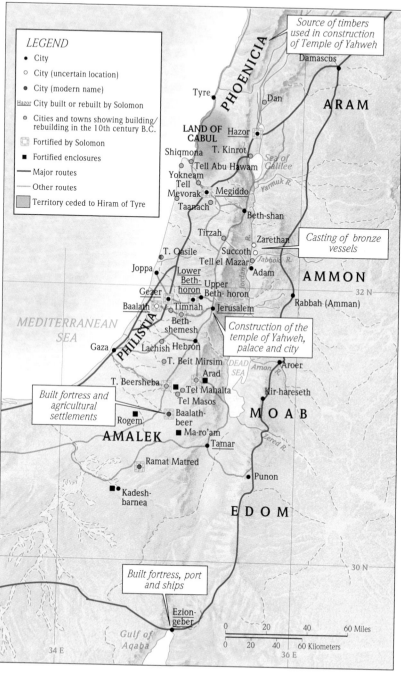

LEGEND

- City
- ○ City (uncertain location)
- ● City (modern name)
- Hazor City built or rebuilt by Solomon
- ◉ Cities and towns showing building/ rebuilding in the 10th century B.C.
- ▢ Fortified by Solomon
- ■ Fortified enclosures
- ── Major routes
- ── Other routes
- Territory ceded to Hiram of Tyre

PHOENICIA

ARAM

Source of timbers used in construction of Temple of Yahweh

Damascus

Tyre
Dan

LAND OF CABUL
Hazor
Shiqmona
T. Kinrot
Sea of Galilee

Tell Abu Hawam
Yokneam
Tell Mevorak
Megiddo
Yarmuk R.
Taanach
Beth-shan

Tirzah
Zarethan
T. Qasile
Succoth
Casting of bronze vessels

Joppa
Tell el Mazar
Adam
Jabbok R.
AMMON

Lower Beth-horon
Upper Beth-horon
32 N
Gezer
Jerusalem
Rabbah (Amman)
Baalath
Timnah

MEDITERRANEAN SEA
PHILISTIA
Beth-shemesh
Construction of the temple of Yahweh, palace and city

Gaza
Lachish Hebron
T. Beit Mirsim
(DEAD) SEA
Arnon
Aroer
T. Beersheba
Arad
Kir-hareseth
Tel Mahalta
Built fortress and agricultural settlements
Tel Masos
Rogem
Baalath-beer
MOAB
AMALEK
Ma-ro'am
Tamar
Zered R.

Ramat Matred

Punon

Kadesh-barnea
EDOM

30 N

Built fortress, port and ships

Ezion-geber

Gulf of Aqaba
34 E
0   20   40   60 Miles
0   20   40   60 Kilometers
36 E

1 Kings 6:1

In the four hundred and eightieth year after the Israelites had come out of Egypt, in the fourth year of Solomon's reign over Israel, in the month of Ziv, the second month, he began to build the temple of the LORD.

44 ▶ JERUSALEM IN THE TIME OF DAVID AND SOLOMON

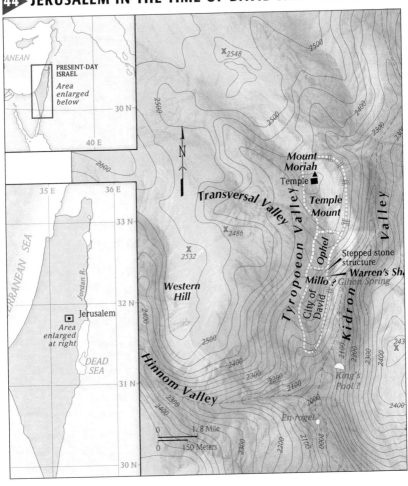

2 Chronicles 3:1-2

Then Solomon began to build the temple of the LORD in Jerusalem on Mount Moriah, where the LORD had appeared to his father David. It was on the threshing floor of Araunah the Jebusite, the place provided by David. He began building on the second day of the second month in the fourth year of his reign.

45 THE KINGDOMS OF ISRAEL AND JUDAH

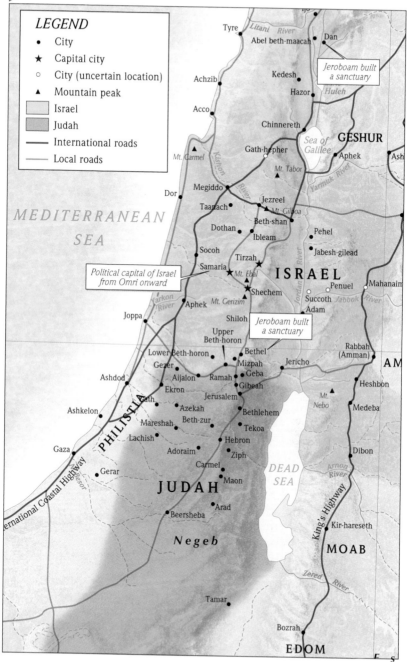

LEGEND
- • City
- ★ Capital city
- ○ City (uncertain location)
- ▲ Mountain peak
-   Israel
-   Judah
- ── International roads
- ── Local roads

Jeroboam built a sanctuary

Political capital of Israel from Omri onward

Jeroboam built a sanctuary

1 Kings 12:26-27

Jeroboam thought to himself, "The kingdom will now likely revert to the house of David. If these people go up to offer sacrifices at the temple of the LORD in Jerusalem, they will again give their allegiance to their lord, Rehoboam king of Judah. They will kill me and return to King Rehoboam."

46 THE CAMPAIGN OF SHISHAK AND REHOBOAM'S DEFENSE LINES

LEGEND
- • City
- ○ City (uncertain location)
- ◉ City (fortified by Rehoboam)
- ⊕ City (archaeological evidence, but ancient name uncertain)
- ▲ Mountain peak
- Israel
- Judah
- ← Shishak's campaign

2 Chronicles 12:2
Because they had been unfaithful to the LORD, Shishak king of Egypt attacked Jerusalem in the fifth year of King Rehoboam.

47 CONFLICTS BETWEEN ISRAEL AND ARAM-DAMASCUS

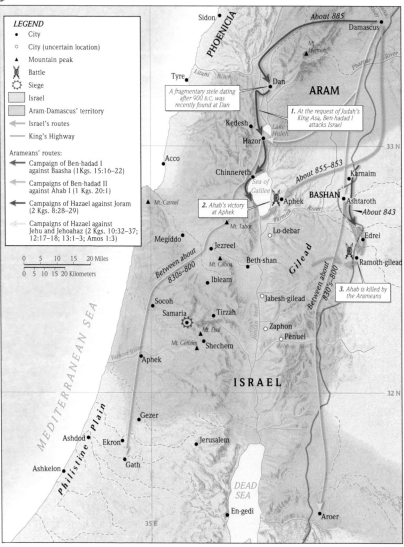

LEGEND

- • City
- ○ City (uncertain location)
- ▲ Mountain peak
- ⚔ Battle
- ⚙ Siege
- ▢ Israel
- ▢ Aram-Damascus' territory
- ← Israel's routes
- — King's Highway

Arameans' routes:
- ◄ Campaign of Ben-hadad I against Baasha (1 Kgs. 15:16–22)
- ◄ Campaigns of Ben-hadad II against Ahab I (1 Kgs. 20:1)
- ◄ Campaigns of Hazael against Joram (2 Kgs. 8:28–29)
- ◄ Campaigns of Hazael against Jehu and Jehoahaz (2 Kgs. 10:32–37; 12:17–18; 13:1–3; Amos 1:3)

0   5   10   15   20 Miles
0 5 10 15 20 Kilometers

A fragmentary stele dating after 900 B.C. was recently found at Dan

1. At the request of Judah's King Asa, Ben-hadad I attacks Israel

2. Ahab's victory at Aphek

3. Ahab is killed by the Arameans

About 885
About 855–853
About 843
Between about 830s–800
Between about 830s–800

33 N
32 N
35 E

Sidon
PHOENICIA
Damascus
Mt. Hermon ▲
ARAM
Pharpar River
Tyre
Litani River
Dan
Kedesh
Hazor
Lake Huleh
Acco
Chinnereth
Sea of Galilee
Karnaim
BASHAN
Ashtaroth
Aphek
Yarmuk River
Mt. Carmel ▲
Lo-debar
Gilead
Edrei
Megiddo
Jezreel
Mt. Tabor ▲
Beth-shan
Ramoth-gilead
Mt. Gilboa ▲
Ibleam
Jabesh-gilead
Jordan River
Socoh
Samaria ⚙
Tirzah
Zaphon
Penuel
Jabbok River
Mt. Ebal ▲
Mt. Gerizim ▲
Shechem
Aphek
Yarkon River
ISRAEL
MEDITERRANEAN SEA
Gezer
Ashdod
Ekron
Jerusalem
Philistine Plain
Ashkelon
Gath
DEAD SEA
En-gedi
Aroer

2 Kings 8:28

Ahaziah went with Joram son of Ahab to war against Hazael king of Aram at Ramoth Gilead. The Arameans wounded Joram;

48 ▶ THE OMRIDE DYNASTY

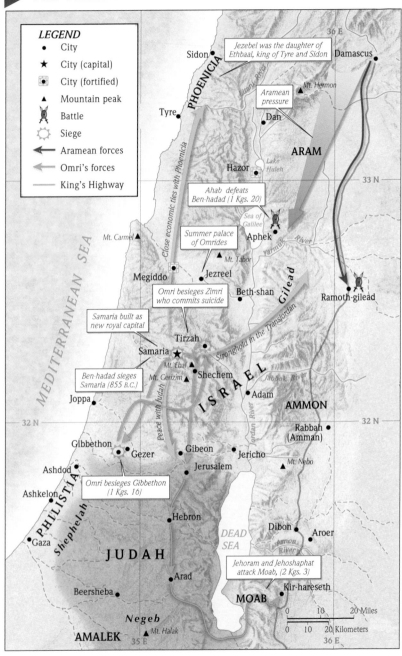

LEGEND
- • City
- ★ City (capital)
- ⊡ City (fortified)
- ▲ Mountain peak
- ⚔ Battle
- ☼ Siege
- ← Aramean forces
- ← Omri's forces
- — King's Highway

Jezebel was the daughter of Ethbaal, king of Tyre and Sidon

Aramean pressure

Ahab defeats Ben-hadad (1 Kgs. 20)

Summer palace of Omrides

Omri besieges Zimri who commits suicide

Samaria built as new royal capital

Ben-hadad sieges Samaria (855 B.C.)

Omri besieges Gibbethon (1 Kgs. 16)

Jehoram and Jehoshaphat attack Moab, (2 Kgs. 3)

1 Kings 16:29-30

In the thirty-eighth year of Asa king of Judah, Ahab son of Omri became king of Israel, and he reigned in Samaria over Israel twenty-two years. Ahab son of Omri did more evil in the eyes of the LORD than any of those before him.

49 ELIJAH AND ELISHA

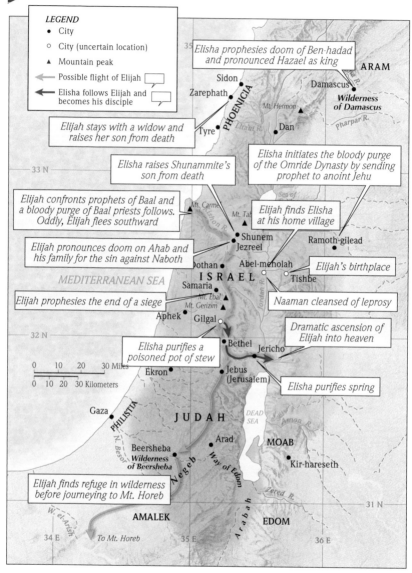

LEGEND
- • City
- ○ City (uncertain location)
- ▲ Mountain peak
- ← Possible flight of Elijah
- ← Elisha follows Elijah and becomes his disciple

Elisha prophesies doom of Ben-hadad and pronounced Hazael as king

Elijah stays with a widow and raises her son from death

Elisha raises Shunammite's son from death

Elijah confronts prophets of Baal and a bloody purge of Baal priests follows. Oddly, Elijah flees southward

Elisha initiates the bloody purge of the Omride Dynasty by sending prophet to anoint Jehu

Elijah finds Elisha at his home village

Elijah pronounces doom on Ahab and his family for the sin against Naboth

Elijah's birthplace

Elijah prophesies the end of a siege

Naaman cleansed of leprosy

Dramatic ascension of Elijah into heaven

Elisha purifies a poisoned pot of stew

Elisha purifies spring

Elijah finds refuge in wilderness before journeying to Mt. Horeb

SIDON, Zarephath, PHOENICIA, Tyre, Mt. Hermon, Dan, Damascus, ARAM, Wilderness of Damascus, Pharpar R., Sea of, Mt. Carmel, Mt. Tab, Shunem, Jezreel, Ramoth-gilead, Dothan, Abel-meholah, Tishbe, MEDITERRANEAN SEA, ISRAEL, Samaria, Mt. Ebal, Mt. Gerizim, Aphek, Gilgal, Bethel, Jericho, Ekron, Jebus (Jerusalem), Gaza, PHILISTIA, JUDAH, DEAD SEA, Arad, MOAB, Beersheba, Wilderness of Beersheba, Negeb, Way of Edom, Kir-hareseth, Zered R., Arnon R., AMALEK, EDOM, Arabah, W. et-Arish, To Mt. Horeb

0 10 20 30 Miles
0 10 20 30 Kilometers

35 N · 33 N · 32 N · 31 N
34 E · 35 E · 36 E

2 Kings 2:1-2

When the LORD was about to take Elijah up to heaven in a whirlwind, Elijah and Elisha were on their way from Gilgal. Elijah said to Elisha, "Stay here; the LORD has sent me to Bethel." But Elisha said, "As surely as the LORD lives and as you live, I will not leave you." So they went down to Bethel.

50 ▶ THE REVOLT OF JEHU

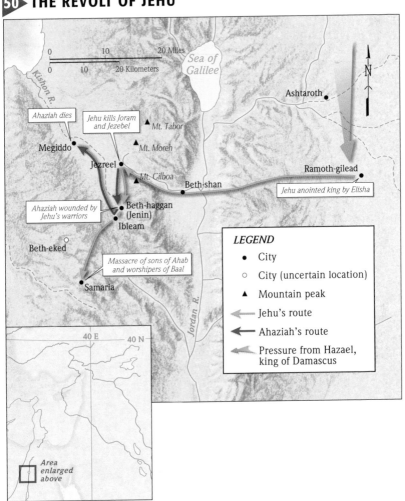

2 Kings 10:17

When Jehu came to Samaria, he killed all who were left there of Ahab's family; he destroyed them, according to the word of the LORD spoken to Elijah.

51 ▶ THE RISE OF ASSYRIA

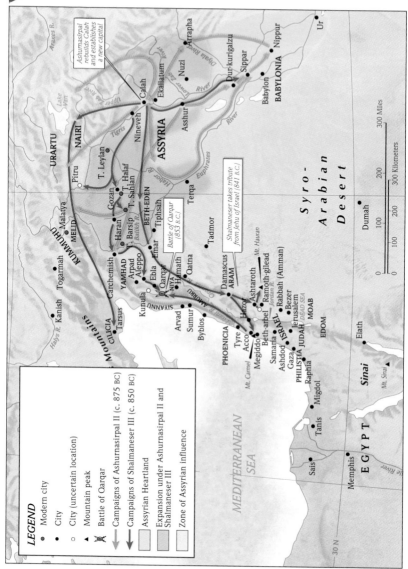

Isaiah 10:5-7
"Woe to the Assyrian, the rod of my anger,
in whose hand is the club of my wrath!
I send him against a godless nation,
I dispatch him against a people who anger me,
to seize loot and snatch plunder,
and to trample them down like mud in the streets.
But this is not what he intends,
this is not what he has in mind;
his purpose is to destroy,
to put an end to many nations.

52 ▶ ISRAEL AND JUDAH IN THE DAYS OF JEROBOAM II AND UZZIAH

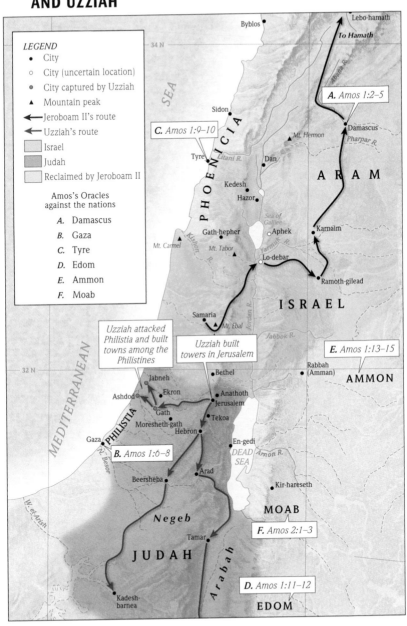

LEGEND
- City
- City (uncertain location)
- City captured by Uzziah
- ▲ Mountain peak
- ← Jeroboam II's route
- ← Uzziah's route
- Israel
- Judah
- Reclaimed by Jeroboam II

Amos's Oracles against the nations

A. Damascus
B. Gaza
C. Tyre
D. Edom
E. Ammon
F. Moab

A. Amos 1:2–5
C. Amos 1:9–10
E. Amos 1:13–15
B. Amos 1:6–8
F. Amos 2:1–3
D. Amos 1:11–12

Uzziah attacked Philistia and built towns among the Philistines

Uzziah built towers in Jerusalem

2 Chronicles 26:6-8
He went to war against the Philistines and broke down the walls of Gath, Jabneh and Ashdod. He then rebuilt towns near Ashdod and elsewhere among the Philistines. God helped him against the Philistines and against the Arabs who lived in Gur Baal and against the Meunites. The Ammonites brought tribute to Uzziah, and his fame spread as far as the border of Egypt, because he had become very powerful.

53▶ THE ASSYRIAN EMPIRE UNDER TIGLATH-PILESER III

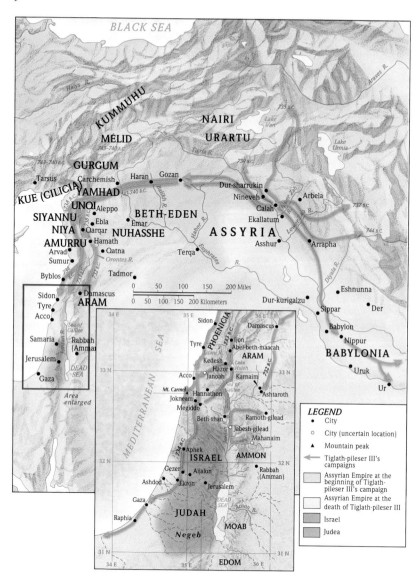

2 Kings 15:19-20

Then Pul king of Assyria invaded the land, and Menahem gave him a thousand talents of silver to gain his support and strengthen his own hold on the kingdom. Menahem exacted this money from Israel. Every wealthy man had to contribute fifty shekels of silver to be given to the king of Assyria. So the king of Assyria withdrew and stayed in the land no longer.

54 THE SYRO-EPHRAIMITE WAR

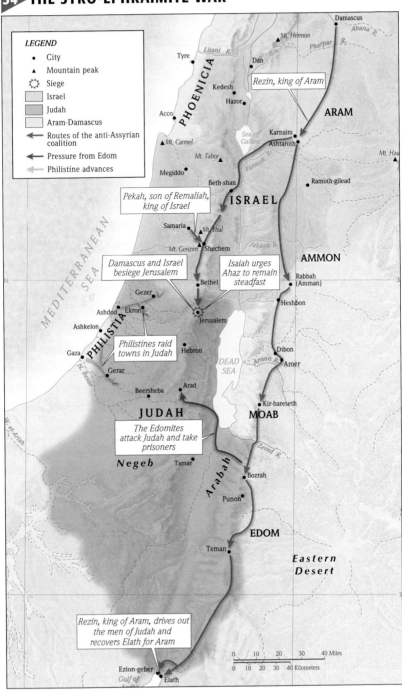

Isaiah 7:1

When Ahaz son of Jotham, the son of Uzziah, was king of Judah, King Rezin of Aram and Pekah son of Remaliah king of Israel marched up to fight against Jerusalem, but they could not overpower it.

55 TIGLATH-PILESER III'S CAMPAIGNS

LEGEND
- City
- City (uncertain location)
- City mentioned in 2 Kgs 15:29
- ▲ Mountain peak
- ← Tiglath-pileser III (734 B.C.) (campaign against the Philistines)
- ← Tiglath-pileser III (733 B.C.) (campaign against Israel)
- ← Tiglath-pileser III (732 B.C.) (campaign against Damascus)
- **TYRE** Assyrian province

2 Kings 16:10
Then King Ahaz went to Damascus to meet Tiglath-Pileser king of Assyria. He saw an altar in Damascus and sent to Uriah the priest a sketch of the altar, with detailed plans for its construction.

56▶ THE FALL OF SAMARIA AND DEPORTATION OF ISRAELITES

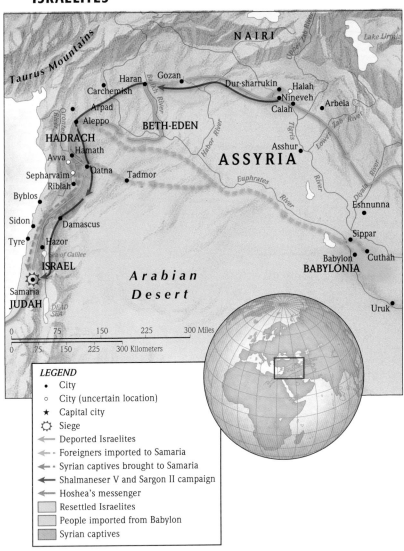

2 Kings 17:5-7

The king of Assyria invaded the entire land, marched against Samaria and laid siege to it for three years. In the ninth year of Hoshea, the king of Assyria captured Samaria and deported the Israelites to Assyria. He settled them in Halah, in Gozan on the Habor River and in the towns of the Medes. All this took place because the Israelites had sinned against the LORD their God, who had brought them up out of Egypt from under the power of Pharaoh king of Egypt. They worshiped other gods.

57 ASSYRIAN DISTRICTS AFTER THE FALL OF SAMARIA

LEGEND
- City
- Modern city

TYRE Assyrian Districts

Assyrian vassal states

Semi-independent states

Carchemish
T. Barsip

CALNEH Arpad **ARPAD**

Aleppo

HADRACH Emar

Qarqar

SIMYRA **HAMATH**

Arvad Hamath

Qatna

Simyra

SUBITE (ZOBAH)

GUBLA (BYBLOS) Tadmor

Byblos

MEDITERRANEAN SEA

SIDON **DAMASCUS**

Sidon

Damascus

Tyre Dan

TYRE
Kedesh

Acco Hazor

KARNAIM

MEGIDDO Karnaim

Megiddo Ashtaroth

Dor **HAURAN**

DOR Socoh Beth-shan Ramoth-gilead

Samaria **GILEAD**

Aphek **SAMARIA**
Joppa
Shiloh Rabbah (Amman)
Azekah Bethel Jericho **AMMON**
Gezer
Ekron Jerusalem Heshbon
Ashdod
Ashkelon Gath Beth-shemesh Medeba
Gaza Hebron Dibon
Lachish En-gedi
Raphia **JUDAH** Adullam **MOAB**
Arad
Beersheba Kir-hareseth

N

Judah remains loyal to Assyria, while Ahaz permits pagan practices to flourish

Eastern Desert

Negeb

ARIBI Bozrah
Kadesh-barnea **EDOM**

0 25 50 75 100 Miles

0 25 50 75 100 Kilometers

2 Kings 17:24

The king of Assyria brought people from Babylon, Cuthah, Avva, Hamath and Sepharvaim and settled them in the towns of Samaria to replace the Israelites. They took over Samaria and lived in its towns.

58 ▶ PROPHETS OF THE EIGHTH CENTURY

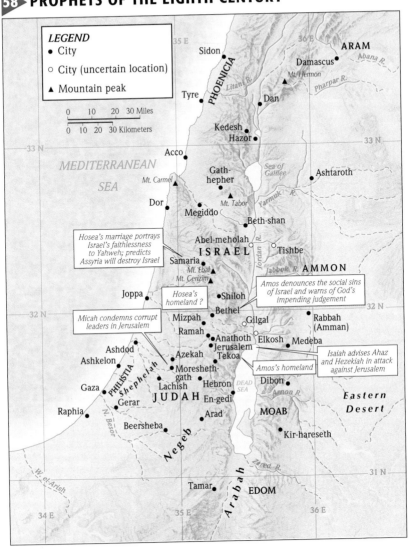

LEGEND
- • City
- ○ City (uncertain location)
- ▲ Mountain peak

0   10   20   30 Miles
0   10   20   30 Kilometers

Hosea's marriage portrays Israel's faithlessness to Yahweh; predicts Assyria will destroy Israel

Amos denounces the social sins of Israel and warns of God's impending judgement

Hosea's homeland ?

Micah condemns corrupt leaders in Jerusalem

Amos's homeland

Isaiah advises Ahaz and Hezekiah in attack against Jerusalem

2 Kings 19:5-7
When King Hezekiah's officials came to Isaiah, Isaiah said to them, "Tell your master, 'This is what the LORD says: Do not be afraid of what you have heard—those words with which the underlings of the king of Assyria have blasphemed me. Listen! I am going to put such a spirit in him that when he hears a certain report, he will return to his own country, and there I will have him cut down with the sword.'"

59► HEZEKIAH'S PREPARATION FOR REVOLT

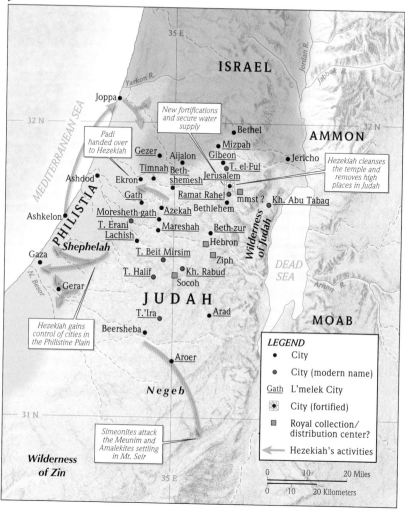

2 Kings 18:1-4

In the third year of Hoshea son of Elah king of Israel, Hezekiah son of Ahaz king of Judah began to reign. He was twenty-five years old when he became king, and he reigned in Jerusalem twenty-nine years. His mother's name was Abijah daughter of Zechariah. He did what was right in the eyes of the LORD, just as his father David had done. He removed the high places, smashed the sacred stones and cut down the Asherah poles. He broke into pieces the bronze snake Moses had made, for up to that time the Israelites had been burning incense to it. (It was called Nehushtan.)

60 ▶ HEZEKIAH'S JERUSALEM

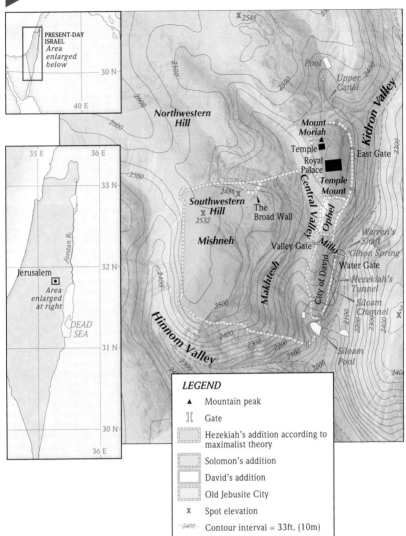

2 Kings 19:32-33
"Therefore this is what the LORD says concerning the king of Assyria:
"He will not enter this city
or shoot an arrow here.
He will not come before it with shield
or build a siege ramp against it.
By the way that he came he will return;
he will not enter this city,
declares the LORD.

61▶ SENNACHERIB'S CAMPAIGN AGAINST JUDAH

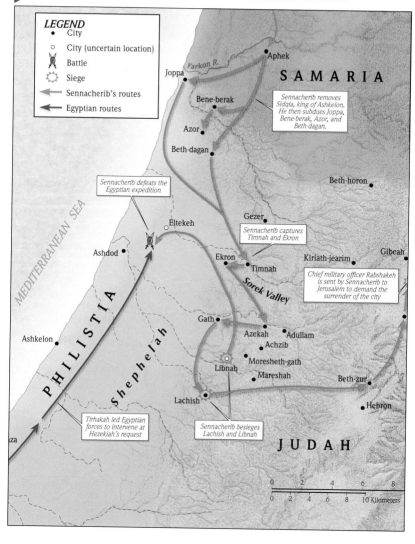

LEGEND
- • City
- ○ City (uncertain location)
- ✖ Battle
- ✿ Siege
- ← Sennacherib's routes
- ← Egyptian routes

Sennacherib removes Sidqia, king of Ashkelon. He then subdues Joppa, Bene-berak, Azor, and Beth-dagan.

Sennacherib defeats the Egyptian expedition

Sennacherib captures Timnah and Ekron

Chief military officer Rabshakeh is sent by Sennacherib to Jerusalem to demand the surrender of the city

Tirhakah led Egyptian forces to intervene at Hezekiah's request

Sennacherib besieges Lachish and Libnah

SAMARIA
PHILISTIA
Shephelah
JUDAH
MEDITERRANEAN SEA
Sorek Valley
Yarkon R.

Aphek, Joppa, Bene-berak, Azor, Beth-dagan, Beth-horon, Gezer, Eltekeh, Ekron, Timnah, Kiriath-jearim, Gibeah, Ashdod, Gath, Azekah, Adullam, Achzib, Libnah, Moresheth-gath, Mareshah, Beth-zur, Ashkelon, Lachish, Hebron, Gaza

0 2 4 6 8
0 2 4 6 8 10 Kilometers

Isaiah 36:1
In the fourteenth year of King Hezekiah's reign, Sennacherib king of Assyria attacked all the fortified cities of Judah and captured them.

62 ASSYRIAN SUPREMACY IN THE SEVENTH CENTURY

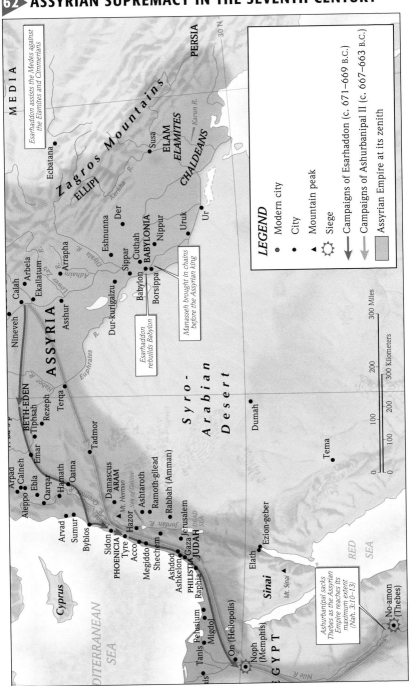

2 Chronicles 33:10-11

The LORD spoke to Manasseh and his people, but they paid no attention. So the LORD brought against them the army commanders of the king of Assyria, who took Manasseh prisoner, put a hook in his nose, bound him with bronze shackles and took him to Babylon.

63 THE RISE OF THE NEO-BABYLONIAN EMPIRE

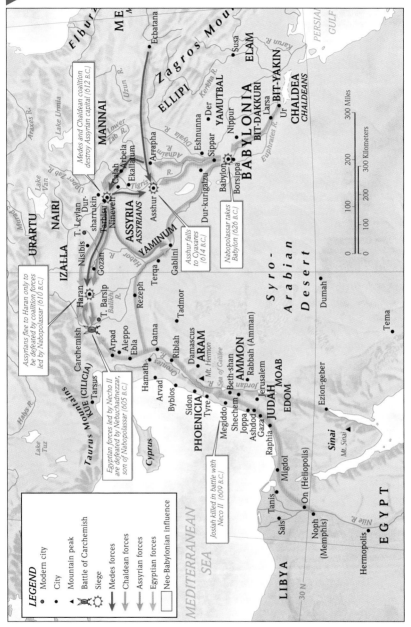

Jeremiah 46:1-2

This is the word of the LORD that came to Jeremiah the prophet concerning the nations:

Concerning Egypt:

This is the message against the army of Pharaoh Neco king of Egypt, which was defeated at Carchemish on the Euphrates River by Nebuchadnezzar king of Babylon in the fourth year of Jehoiakim son of Josiah king of Judah.

64 THE REIGN OF JOSIAH

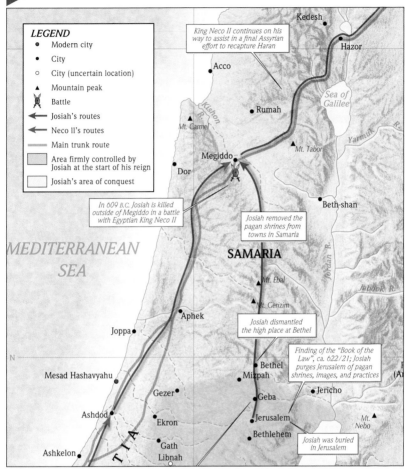

LEGEND
- ● Modern city
- ● City
- ○ City (uncertain location)
- ▲ Mountain peak
- ⚔ Battle
- ← Josiah's routes
- ← Neco ll's routes
- — Main trunk route
- ▨ Area firmly controlled by Josiah at the start of his reign
- ▢ Josiah's area of conquest

King Neco II continues on his way to assist in a final Assyrian effort to recapture Haran

In 609 B.C. Josiah is killed outside of Megiddo in a battle with Egyptian King Neco II

Josiah removed the pagan shrines from towns in Samaria

Josiah dismantled the high place at Bethel

Finding of the "Book of the Law", ca. 622/21; Josiah purges Jerusalem of pagan shrines, images, and practices

Josiah was buried in Jerusalem

Kedesh • Hazor • Acco • Sea of Galilee • Rumah • Mt. Carmel ▲ Kishon • Mt. Tabor ▲ Megiddo • Dor • Beth-shan • Yarmuk R. • Jordan R. • Jabbok R.

MEDITERRANEAN SEA

SAMARIA

Mt. Ebal ▲ • Mt. Gerizim ▲ • Aphek • Joppa • Bethel • Mizpah • Jericho • Mesad Hashavyahu • Gezer • Geba • Jerusalem • Mt. Nebo ▲ • Ashdod • Ekron • Bethlehem • Ashkelon • Gath • Libnah

2 Chronicles 35:20-24

After all this, when Josiah had set the temple in order, Neco king of Egypt went up to fight at Carchemish on the Euphrates, and Josiah marched out to meet him in battle. But Neco sent messengers to him, saying, "What quarrel is there between you and me, O king of Judah? It is not you I am attacking at this time, but the house with which I am at war. God has told me to hurry; so stop opposing God, who is with me, or he will destroy you."

Josiah, however, would not turn away from him, but disguised himself to engage him in battle. He would not listen to what Neco had said at God's command but went to fight him on the plain of Megiddo.

Archers shot King Josiah, and he told his officers, "Take me away; I am badly wounded." So they took him out of his chariot, put him in the other chariot he had and brought him to Jerusalem, where he died. He was buried in the tombs of his fathers, and all Judah and Jerusalem mourned for him.

65 NEBUCHADNEZZAR'S CAMPAIGNS AGAINST JUDAH

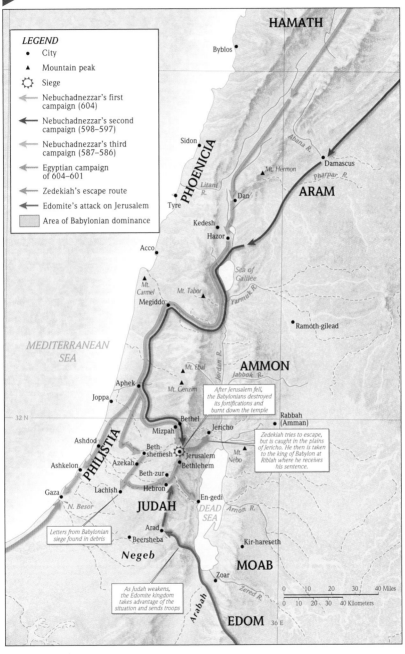

LEGEND
- City
- ▲ Mountain peak
- ☼ Siege
- → Nebuchadnezzar's first campaign (604)
- → Nebuchadnezzar's second campaign (598–597)
- → Nebuchadnezzar's third campaign (587–586)
- → Egyptian campaign of 604–601
- → Zedekiah's escape route
- → Edomite's attack on Jerusalem
- Area of Babylonian dominance

HAMATH

Byblos

Sidon

PHOENICIA

Litani R.

Tyre

Kedesh

Acco

Mt. Carmel

Mt. Tabor

Megiddo

MEDITERRANEAN SEA

Aphek

Joppa

32 N

Ashdod

Ashkelon

Azekah

Beth-shemesh

Gaza

Lachish

N. Besor

Letters from Babylonian siege found in debris

Hebron

Beth-zur

Bethlehem

JUDAH

Arad

Beersheba

Negeb

As Judah weakens, the Edomite kingdom takes advantage of the situation and sends troops

Zoar

Arabah

Zered R.

EDOM 36 E

Mt. Hermon

Damascus

Abana R.

Pharpar R.

ARAM

Dan

Hazor

Sea of Galilee

Yarmuk R.

Ramoth-gilead

Mt. Ebal

Mt. Gerizim

AMMON

Jordan R.

Jabbok R.

Bethel

Mizpah

Jericho

Jerusalem

After Jerusalem fell, the Babylonians destroyed its fortifications and burnt down the temple

Rabbah (Amman)

Zedekiah tries to escape, but is caught in the plains of Jericho. He then is taken to the king of Babylon at Riblah where he receives his sentence.

Mt. Nebo

Arnon R.

DEAD SEA

En-gedi

Kir-hareseth

MOAB

0 10 20 30 40 Miles
0 10 20 30 40 Kilometers

Jeremiah 52:4-5

So in the ninth year of Zedekiah's reign, on the tenth day of the tenth month, Nebuchadnezzar king of Babylon marched against Jerusalem with his whole army. They camped outside the city and built siege works all around it. The city was kept under siege until the eleventh year of King Zedekiah.

66 JUDAH DURING THE EXILE

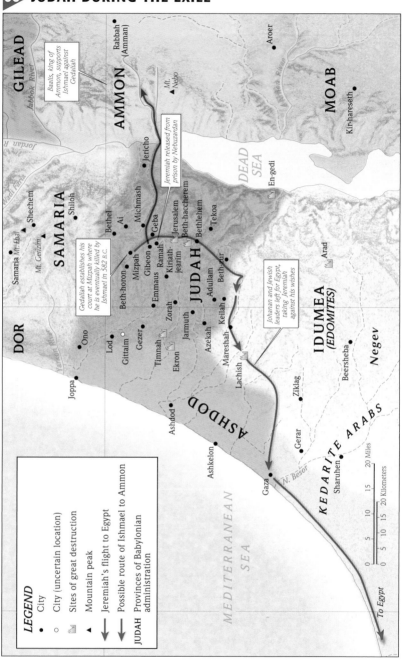

Jeremiah 42:19

"O remnant of Judah, the LORD has told you, 'Do not go to Egypt.' Be sure of this: I warn you today."

67 JEWISH EXILES IN BABYLONIA

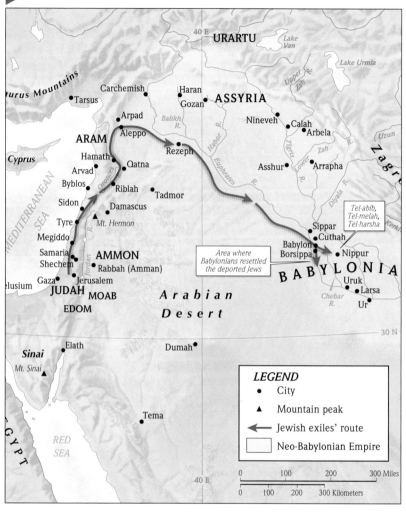

Jeremiah 52:28-30

This is the number of the people Nebuchadnezzar carried into exile: in the seventh year, 3,023 Jews; in Nebuchadnezzar's eighteenth year, 832 people from Jerusalem; in his twenty-third year, 745 Jews taken into exile by Nebuzaradan the commander of the imperial guard. There were 4,600 people in all.

68 ▶ JEWISH REFUGEES IN EGYPT

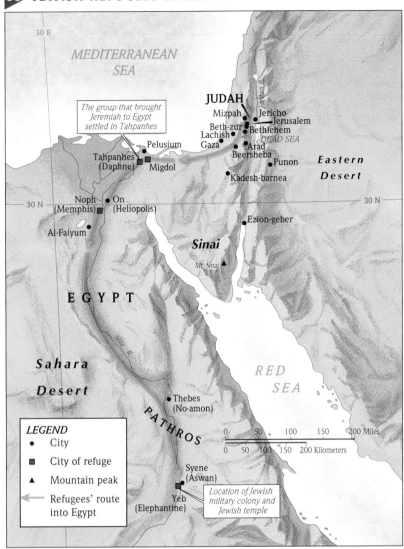

2 Kings 25:25-26

In the seventh month, however, Ishmael son of Nethaniah, the son of Elishama, who was of royal blood, came with ten men and assassinated Gedaliah and also the men of Judah and the Babylonians who were with him at Mizpah. At this, all the people from the least to the greatest, together with the army officers, fled to Egypt for fear of the Babylonians.

69 ▶ THE CONQUESTS OF CYRUS THE GREAT

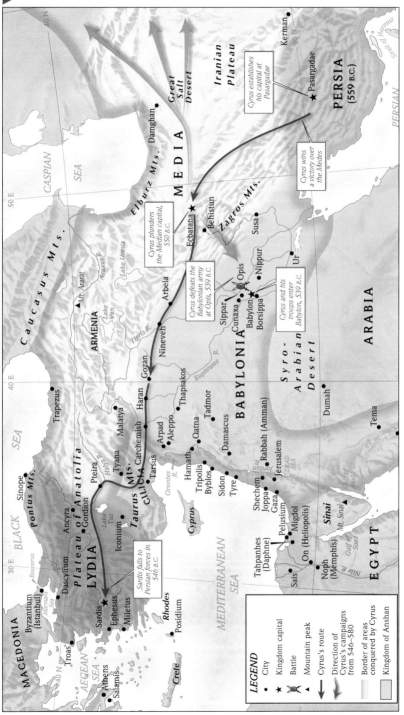

Cyrus establishes his capital at Pasargadae

Cyrus wins a victory over the Medes

Cyrus plunders the Median capital, 550 B.C.

Cyrus defeats the Babylonian army at Opis, 539 B.C.

Cyrus and his troops enter Babylon, 539 B.C.

Sardis falls to Persian forces in 546 B.C.

PERSIA (559 B.C.)

LEGEND
- ● City
- ★ Kingdom capital
- ⚔ Battle
- ▲ Mountain peak
- ↓ Cyrus's route
- ⇓ Direction of Cyrus's campaigns from 546–580
- Border of areas conquered by Cyrus
- Kingdom of Anshan

Isaiah 44:24,28

28 I am the Lord...who says of Cyrus, "he is my shepherd and will accomplish all that I please."

70▶ THE RETURNS OF JEWISH EXILES TO JUDAH

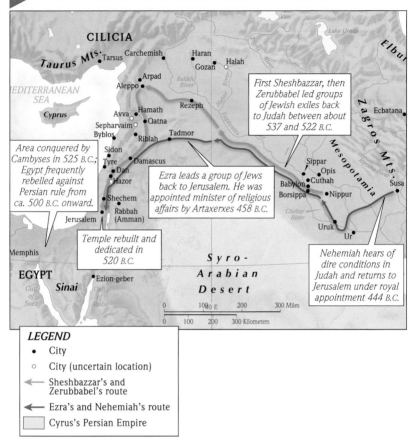

First Sheshbazzar, then Zerubbabel led groups of Jewish exiles back to Judah between about 537 and 522 B.C.

Area conquered by Cambyses in 525 B.C.; Egypt frequently rebelled against Persian rule from ca. 500 B.C. onward.

Ezra leads a group of Jews back to Jerusalem. He was appointed minister of religious affairs by Artaxerxes 458 B.C.

Temple rebuilt and dedicated in 520 B.C.

Nehemiah hears of dire conditions in Judah and returns to Jerusalem under royal appointment 444 B.C.

LEGEND
- • City
- ○ City (uncertain location)
- ← Sheshbazzar's and Zerubbabel's route
- ← Ezra's and Nehemiah's route
- ▢ Cyrus's Persian Empire

Ezra 1:2-4

"This is what Cyrus king of Persia says:

"'The LORD, the God of heaven, has given me all the kingdoms of the earth and he has appointed me to build a temple for him at Jerusalem in Judah. Anyone of his people among you-may his God be with him, and let him go up to Jerusalem in Judah and build the temple of the LORD , the God of Israel, the God who is in Jerusalem. And the people of any place where survivors may now be living are to provide him with silver and gold, with goods and livestock, and with freewill offerings for the temple of God in Jerusalem.'"

71 ▶ THE PROVINCE OF JUDAH AND NEHEMIAH'S ENEMIES IN THE FIFTH CENTURY

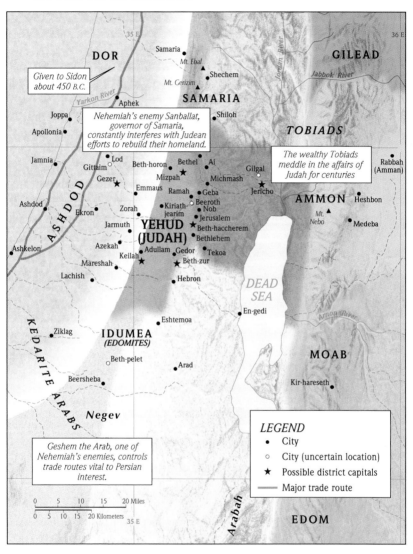

Nehemiah 4:6-8

So we rebuilt the wall till all of it reached half its height, for the people worked with all their heart. But when Sanballat, Tobiah, the Arabs, the Ammonites and the men of Ashdod heard that the repairs to Jerusalem's walls had gone ahead and that the gaps were being closed, they were very angry. They all plotted together to come and fight against Jerusalem and stir up trouble against it.

72 ALEXANDER THE GREAT'S EMPIRE

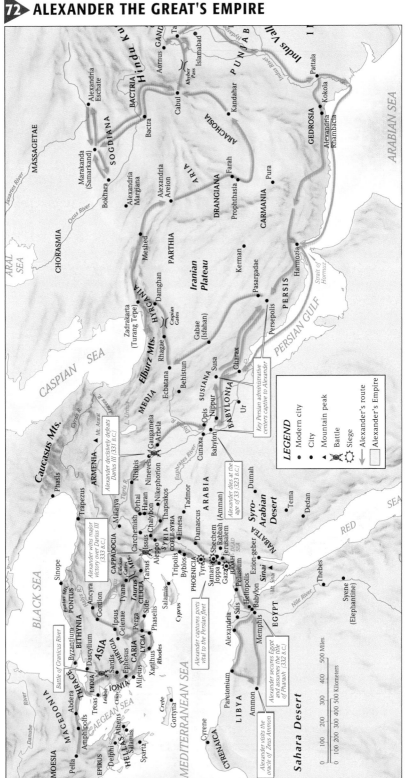

73 THE ROMAN EMPIRE IN THE AGE OF AUGUSTUS

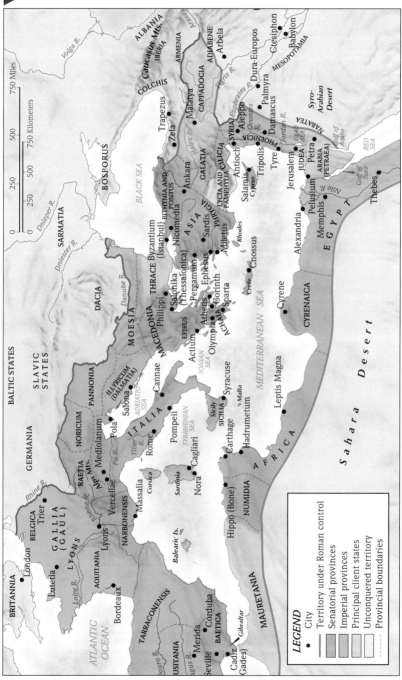

Luke 2:1-3

In those days a decree went out from Caesar Augustus that the whole empire should be registered. This first registration took place while Quirinius was governing Syria. So everyone went to be registered, each to his own town.

74▶ ROMAN RULE IN PALESTINE

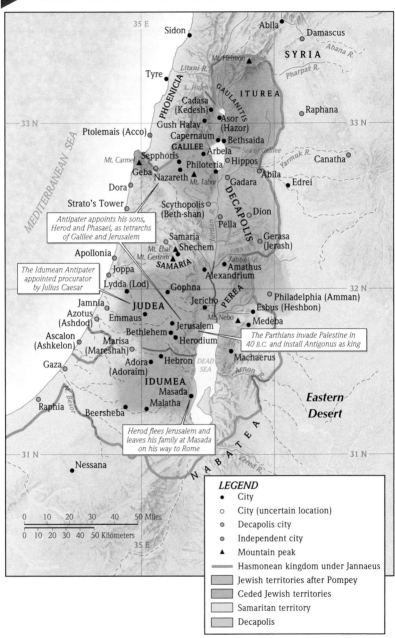

75 THE KINGDOM OF HEROD THE GREAT

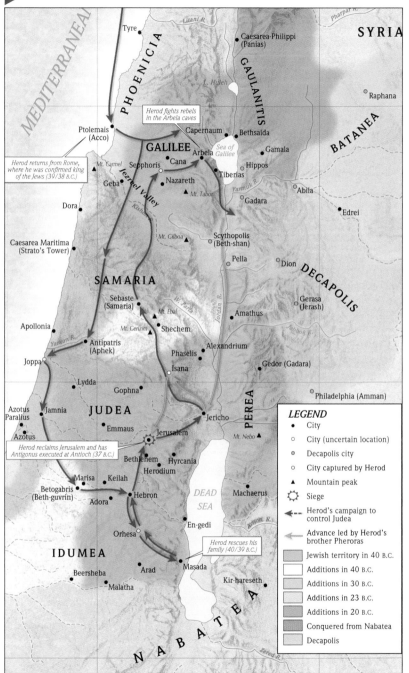

Matthew 2:1-2

After Jesus was born in Bethlehem of Judea in the days of King Herod, wise men from the east arrived unexpectedly in Jerusalem, saying, "Where is He who has been born King of the Jews? For we saw His star in the east and have come to worship Him."

76 ► HEROD'S BUILDING PROGRAM

LEGEND
- • City
- ◉ Decapolis city
- ▣ Site of Herod's building program or military installation
- ▲ Mountain peak
- Herod's kingdom

Great port that linked Palestine with the Roman Empire

Samaria was rebuilt as Sebaste to honor Augustus

Herod's main palace and extravagent new temple were located in Jerusalem

Herod's royal retreat

Herod's cone-shaped mountain fortress

Herod's rock fortress built on a 1,300 ft. mesa above the Dead Sea shore

MEDITERRANEAN SEA
33 N

PHOENICIA
ITUREA
Mt. Hermon ▲
36 E
ABILENE
Damascus ◉
Abana R.
Pharpar R.
SYRIA
Caesarea-Philippi (Panias) ▣
GAULANITIS
Cadasa (Kedesh) ▣ Ijon
Raphana ◉
33 N
Ptolemais (Acco) •
Gush Halav •
GALILEE
Bethsaida ▣
BATANEA
TRACHONITIS
Mt. Carmel ▲
Sepphoris ▣
Arbela ▣
Sea of Galilee
Gamala •
Hippos ◉
Canatha ◉
Geba •
Mt. Tabor ▲
Yarmuk R.
Abila ◉
Dora •
Nazareth •
Gadara ◉
Adraa (Edrei) •
AURANITIS
Agrippina
Caesarea Maritima ▣
Scythopolis (Beth-shan) ◉
Pella ◉
Dion ◉
Narbata •
SAMARIA
Jordan R.
DECAPOLIS
Sebaste (Samaria) ▣
Amathus ▣
Apollonia •
Mt. Ebal ▲
Jabbok R.
Gerasa (Jerash) ◉
Qiryat Bene Hassan ▣
Mt. Gerizim ▲
Shechem •
Joppa •
Antipatris (Aphek) ▣
Alexandrium (Sartaba) ▣
Phasaelis ▣
Gedor (Gadara) ▣
32 N
PEREA
Threx ▣
Doc (Docus) ▣
Philadelphia (Amman) ◉
Azotus (Ashdod) •
Cypros ▣
Jericho ▣
Esbus (Heshbon) ▣
Emmaus •
Jerusalem ▣
Livias (Beth-ramatha) ▣
Ascalon (Ashkelon) •
Marisa (Mareshah) ▣
JUDEA
Medeba •
Hyrcania ▣
Herodium ▣
Gaza •
Betogabris (Beth-guvrin) ▣
Hebron ▣
Machaerus ▣
Callirrhoe (Zereth-shahar) •
IDUMEA
DEAD SEA
Eastern Desert
Raphia •
Masada ▣
Beersheba •
Malatha •
NABATEA
31 N
Nessana •
Zered R.
Khirbet Tannur •
31 N

0 10 20 30 40 50 Miles
0 10 20 30 40 50 Kilometers
35 E
36 E

Arabah
N. Besor

77 THE DIVISION OF HEROD'S KINGDOM

LEGEND
- City
- Decapolis city
- Decapolis city (uncertain location)
- ▲ Mountain peak
- To Antipas
- To Archelaus
- To Philip
- To Salome
- Syrian province

ITUREA

Sidon

Mt. Hermon ▲

Litani R.

Pharpar

Tyre

PHOENICIA

Caesarea-Philippi (Panias)

GAULANITIS

Cadasa (Kedesh)

Gischala (Gush Halav)

Huleh

BATANEA

Ptolemais (Acco)

Capernaum

Bethsaida

Sea of Galilee

Gamala

Jotapata Gabara

Taricheae

Mt. Carmel ▲

GALILEE

Arbela

Hippos

Geba

Sepphoris Nazareth

Tiberias

Yarmuk R.

Abila

Mt. Tabor ▲

Philoteria (Beth-Yerah)

Gadara

Dora

Adraa (Edrei)

MEDITERRANEAN SEA

Caesarea Maritima (Strato's Tower)

Ginae (Jenin)

Scythopolis (Beth-shan)

DECAPOLIS

Narbata

Pella

Dion

SAMARIA

Jordan R.

Gerasa (Jerash)

Sebaste (Samaria)

Mt. Ebal

Amathus

Apollonia

Mt. Gerizim ▲

Neapolis (Shechem)

Jabbok R.

Antipatris (Aphek)

Alexandrium (Sartaba)

Joppa

Phasaelis

Gedor (Gadara)

Aphairema (Ophrah)

PEREA

Lydda

Gophna

Archelais

Philadelphia (Amman)

JUDEA

Threx

Doc (Docus)

Jamnia

Emmaus (Nicopolis)

Jericho

Esbus (Heshbon)

Azotus (Ashdod)

Cypros

Livias (Beth-ramatha)

Mt. Nebo ▲

lon on)

Jerusalem

Medeba

Hyrcania

edon

Betogabris (Beth-guvrin)

Marisa (Mareshah)

Herodium

Machaerus

aza

Hebron

Callirrhoe (Zereth-shahar)

DEAD SEA

Arnon R.

IDUMEA

Masada

N. Besor

Beersheba

Arad

NABATEA

Malatha

78 ▶ PALESTINE IN THE TIME OF JESUS

LEGEND
- City
- City (uncertain location)
- Decapolis city
- Decapolis city (uncertain location)
- ★ Administrative capital
- ▲ Mountain peak
- — Major roads
- — Other roads
- First procuratorship
- Territory of Antipas
- Territory of Philip
- Syrian territory

Coponius was named the first prefect and established the administrative capital at Caesarea Maritima

79 ▶ JESUS' BIRTH AND EARLY CHILDHOOD

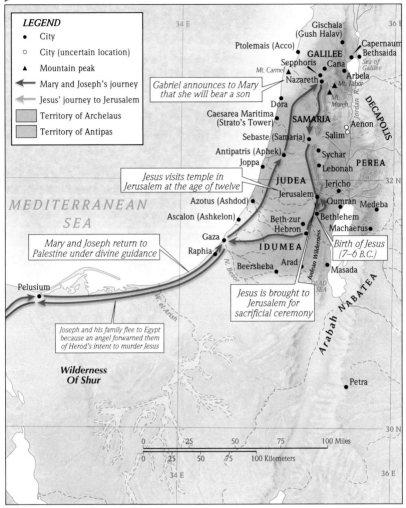

LEGEND
- • City
- ○ City (uncertain location)
- ▲ Mountain peak
- ← Mary and Joseph's journey
- ← Jesus' journey to Jerusalem
- ▨ Territory of Archelaus
- ▨ Territory of Antipas

34 E   36 E

Gischala (Gush Halav)
Capernaum
Ptolemais (Acco)
Bethsaida
GALILEE
Sepphoris   Cana
Mt. Carmel ▲   Arbela
Nazareth ●   ▲ Mt. Tabor
Sea of Galilee

Gabriel announces to Mary that she will bear a son

Dora
Mt. Moreh
Caesarea Maritima (Strato's Tower)
SAMARIA
Aenon
Salim
Sebaste (Samaria)
Antipatris (Aphek)
Sychar
Joppa
PEREA
Lebonah
JUDEA
Jericho

Jesus visits temple in Jerusalem at the age of twelve

Jerusalem
32 N
Azotus (Ashdod) ●
Qumran
Medeba

MEDITERRANEAN SEA

Ascalon (Ashkelon) ●
Beth-zur ●
Bethlehem
Hebron
Machaerus ●

Mary and Joseph return to Palestine under divine guidance

Gaza
IDUMEA
Birth of Jesus (7–6 B.C.)
Raphia ●
Beersheba
Arad
Masada
N. el-Arish
N. Besor
Judean Wilderness
DEAD SEA

Jesus is brought to Jerusalem for sacrificial ceremony

Pelusium

Arabah NABATEA

Joseph and his family flee to Egypt because an angel forwarned them of Herod's intent to murder Jesus

Wilderness Of Shur

Petra

30 N

0   25   50   75   100 Miles
0   25   50   75   100 Kilometers

34 E   36 E

Luke 2:4-5
And Joseph also went up from the town of Nazareth in Galilee, to Judea, to the city of David, which is called Bethlehem, because he was of the house and family line of David, to be registered along with Mary, who was engaged to him and was pregnant.

80 ▶ JOHN THE BAPTIZER

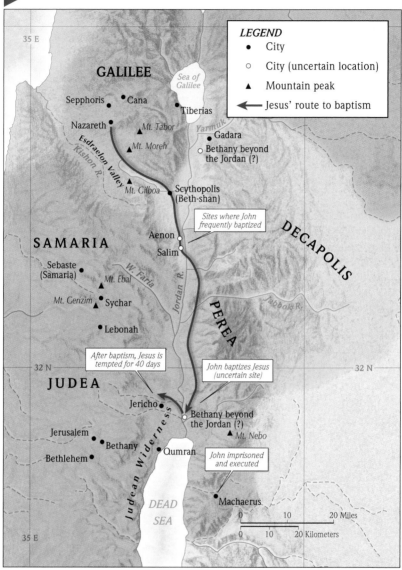

Mark 1:4-5

John came baptizing in the wilderness and preaching a baptism of repentance for the forgiveness of sins. The whole Judean countryside and all the people of Jerusalem were flocking to him, and they were baptized by him in the Jordan River as they confessed their sins.

81 ▶ GALILEE IN THE TIME OF JESUS

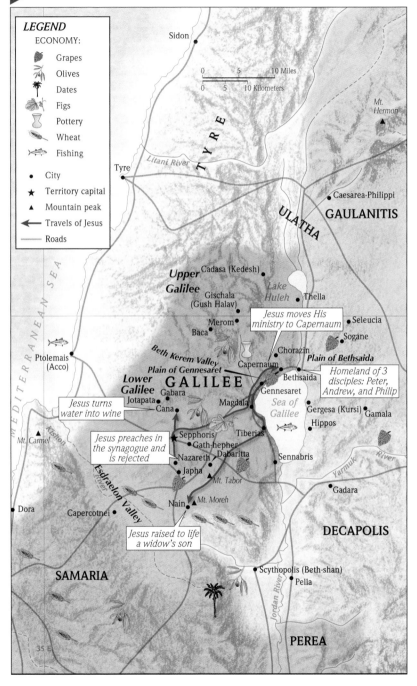

LEGEND
ECONOMY:

- Grapes
- Olives
- Dates
- Figs
- Pottery
- Wheat
- Fishing

- • City
- ★ Territory capital
- ▲ Mountain peak
- ← Travels of Jesus
- — Roads

Sidon

0   5   10 Miles
0   5   10 Kilometers

TYRE

Tyre

Litani River

Mt. Hermon

ULATHA

Caesarea-Philippi

GAULANITIS

Upper Galilee

Cadasa (Kedesh)

Lake Huleh

Thella

Gischala (Gush Halav)

Merom

Baca

Seleucia

Sogane

Jesus moves His ministry to Capernaum

Chorazin

Capernaum

Plain of Bethsaida

Beth Kerem Valley

Plain of Gennesaret

Bethsaida

Ptolemais (Acco)

Lower Galilee

GALILEE

Gabara

Gennesaret

Homeland of 3 disciples: Peter, Andrew, and Philip

MEDITERRANEAN SEA

Jotapata

Cana

Jesus turns water into wine

Magdala

Sea of Galilee

Gergesa (Kursi)

Gamala

Hippos

Sepphoris

Tiberias

Mt. Carmel

Kishon River

Jesus preaches in the synagogue and is rejected

Gath-hepher

Dabaritta

Nazareth

Sennabris

Yarmuk River

Japha

Mt. Tabor

Gadara

Esdraelon Valley

Dora

Capercotnei

Nain

Mt. Moreh

Jesus raised to life a widow's son

DECAPOLIS

SAMARIA

Scythopolis (Beth-shan)

Pella

Jordan River

35 E

PEREA

John 2:1-2
On the third day a wedding took place in Cana of Galilee. Jesus' mother was there, and Jesus and His disciples were invited to the wedding as well.

82▶ THE MINISTRY OF JESUS AROUND THE SEA OF GALILEE

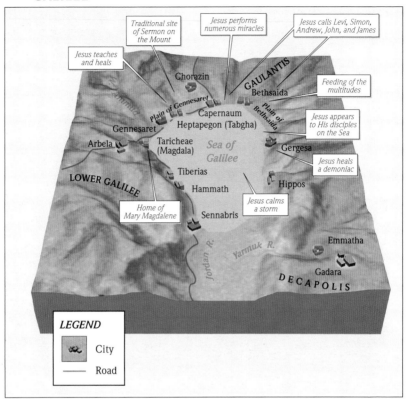

Luke 5:1-2

As the crowd was pressing in on Jesus to hear God's word, He was standing by Lake Gennesaret. He saw two boats at the edge of the lake; the fishermen had left them and were washing their nets.

83 ▶ THE MINISTRY OF JESUS BEYOND GALILEE

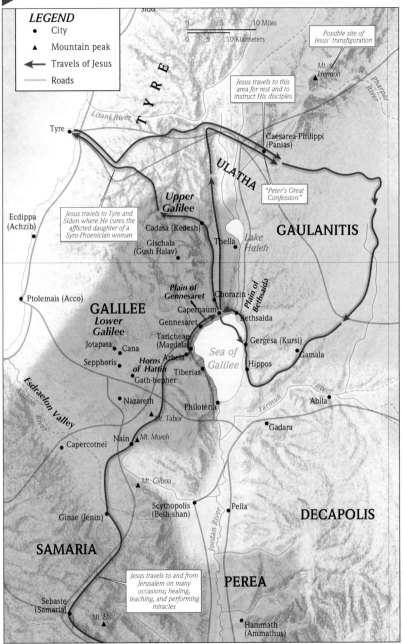

Mark 7:24-26

From there He got up and departed to the region of Tyre and Sidon. He entered a house and did not want anyone to know it, but He could not escape notice. Instead, immediately after hearing about Him, a woman whose little daughter had an unclean spirit came and fell at His feet. Now the woman was Greek, a Syrophoenician by birth, and she kept asking Him to drive the demon out of her daughter.

84 JESUS' JOURNEYS FROM GALILEE TO JUDEA

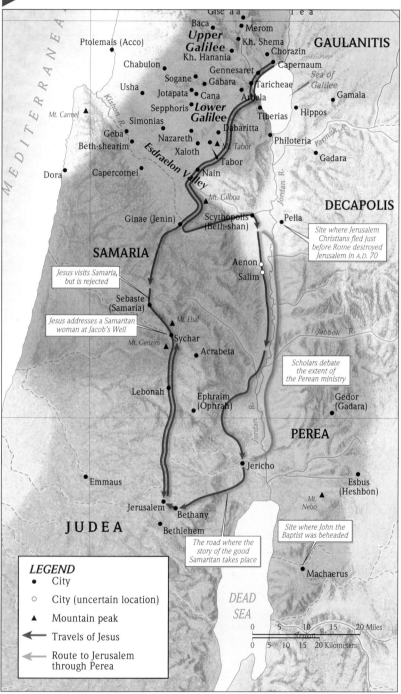

John 4:3-5

He left Judea and went again to Galilee. He had to travel through Samaria, so He came to a town of Samaria called Sychar near the property that Jacob had given his son Joseph.

85 JESUS IN JUDEA AND JERUSALEM

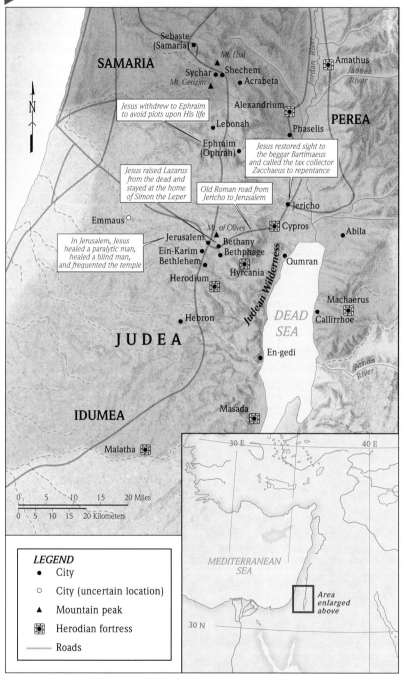

Sebaste
(Samaria)

SAMARIA

Mt. Ebal

Sychar • Shechem
Mt. Gerizim • Acrabela

Amathus
Jabbok River

Jordan River

Alexandrium

PEREA

*Jesus withdrew to Ephraim
to avoid plots upon His life*

Lebonah

Phaselis

Ephraim
(Ophrah)

*Jesus restored sight to
the beggar Bartimaeus
and called the tax collector
Zacchaeus to repentance*

*Jesus raised Lazarus
from the dead and
stayed at the home
of Simon the Leper*

*Old Roman road from
Jericho to Jerusalem*

Jericho

Emmaus

Mt. of Olives

Cypros

Abila

*In Jerusalem, Jesus
healed a paralytic man,
healed a blind man,
and frequented the temple*

Jerusalem
Ein-Karim • Bethany
Bethlehem • Bethphage

Judean Wilderness

Qumran

Herodium

Hyrcania

Machaerus

**DEAD
SEA**

Callirrhoe

Hebron

J U D E A

En-gedi

Arnon River

IDUMEA

Masada

Malatha

0   5   10   15   20 Miles
0   5   10   15   20 Kilometers

30 E

40 E

MEDITERRANEAN
SEA

Area
enlarged
above

30 N

LEGEND
- • City
- ○ City (uncertain location)
- ▲ Mountain peak
- ▣ Herodian fortress
- ----- Roads

Luke 19:1-2
He entered Jericho and was passing through. There was a man
named Zacchaeus who was a chief tax collector, and he was rich.

86 JERUSALEM IN THE NEW TESTAMENT PERIOD

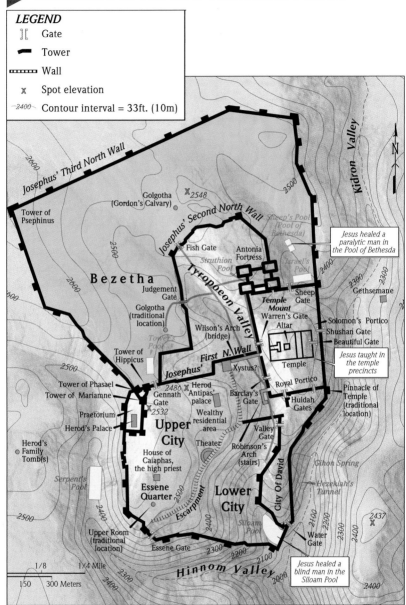

LEGEND

- ⊐⊏ Gate
- ➤ Tower
- ⬜⬜⬜ Wall
- x Spot elevation
- 2400 Contour interval = 33ft. (10m)

Josephus' Third North Wall

Kidron Valley

N

Tower of Psephinus

Golgotha (Gordon's) Calvary   x 2548

Josephus' Second North Wall

Sheep's Pool (Pool of Bethesda)

Jesus healed a paralytic man in the Pool of Bethesda

Fish Gate   Antonia Fortress

Struthion Pool

Israel's Pool

Bezetha

Judgement Gate

Tyropoeon Valley

Temple Mount   Sheep Gate   Gethsemane

Golgotha (traditional location)

Warren's Gate   Solomon's Portico

Wilson's Arch (bridge)   Altar   Shushan Gate

Beautiful Gate

Tower of Hippicus

Tower Pool

First N. Wall

Josephus'

Xystus?   Temple

Jesus taught in the temple precincts

Royal Portico

Pinnacle of Temple (traditional location)

Tower of Phasael

Tower of Mariamne

2486 x Herod Antipas' palace

Gennath Gate   2532

Barclay's Gate

Huldah Gates

Praetorium

Wealthy residential area

Herod's Palace

Upper City

Theater   Valley Gate

Herod's Family Tomb(s)

House of Caiaphas, the high priest

Robinson's Arch (stairs)

City Of David

Gihon Spring

Serpent's Pool

Essene Quarter

Lower City

Hezekiah's Tunnel

2500

Escarpment

Siloam Pool

Water Gate   2437 x

Upper Room (traditional location)

Essene Gate

Hinnom Valley

Jesus healed a blind man in the Siloam Pool

1/8   1/4 Mile

1/50   300 Meters

John 5:1-2

After this a Jewish festival took place, and Jesus went up to Jerusalem. By the Sheep Gate in Jerusalem there is a pool, called Bethesda in Hebrew, which has five colonnades.

87 ▶ THE PASSION WEEK IN JERUSALEM

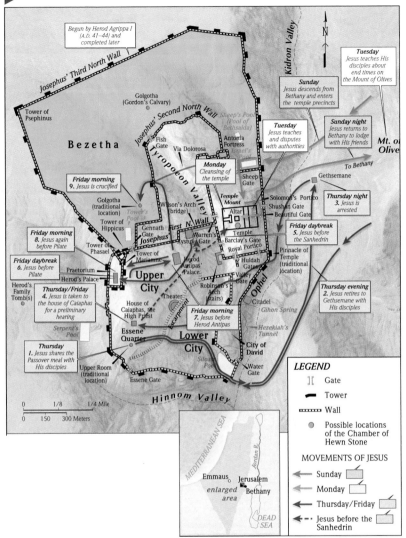

Luke 19:41-44

As He approached and saw the city, He wept over it, saying, "If you knew this day what leads to peace—but now it is hidden from your eyes. For the days will come upon you when your enemies will build an embankment against you, surround you, and hem you in on every side. They will crush you and your children within you to the ground, and they will not leave one stone on another in you, because you did not recognize the time of your visitation.

88 ▶ THE KINGDOM OF HEROD AGRIPPA I

LEGEND
- • City
- ◉ Decapolis city
- ○ Decapolis city (uncertain location)
- ▲ Mountain peak
- ☐ Agrippa's kingdom A.D. 37
- ☐ Agrippa's kingdom A.D. 40
- ☐ Agrippa's kingdom A.D. 41
- ☐ Agrippa's kingdom A.D. 44
- ☐ Kingdom of Chalcis

Ruled by Herod, brother of Agrippa

KINGDOM OF CHALCIS

Gaius Caligula endowment in A.D. 37

Agrippa dies at Caesarea in A.D. 44

Caligula's addition to the kingdom in A.D. 40

Claudius's expansion of Agrippa's lands in A.D. 41

Acts 12:20

He had been very angry with the Tyrians and Sidonians. Together they presented themselves before him, and having won over Blastus, who was in charge of the king's bedroom, they asked for peace, because their country was supplied with food from the king's country.

89 ▶ SECOND PROCURATORSHIP AND THE KINGDOM OF AGRIPPA II

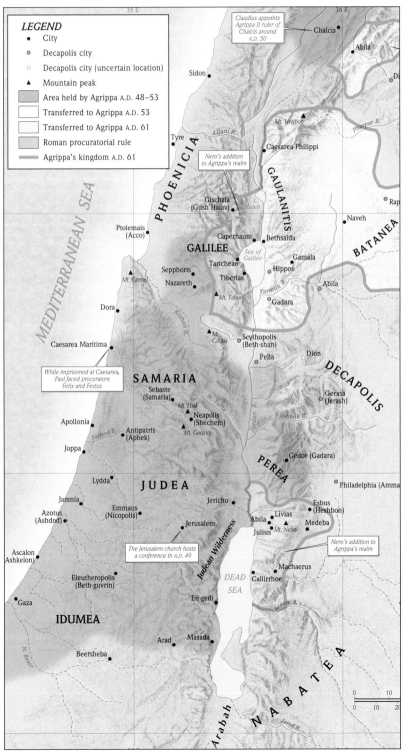

LEGEND

- • City
- ◉ Decapolis city
- ○ Decapolis city (uncertain location)
- ▲ Mountain peak
- Area held by Agrippa A.D. 48–53
- Transferred to Agrippa A.D. 53
- Transferred to Agrippa A.D. 61
- Roman procuratorial rule
- Agrippa's kingdom A.D. 61

Claudius appoints Agrippa II ruler of Chalcis around A.D. 50

Nero's addition to Agrippa's realm

While imprisoned at Caesarea, Paul faced procurators Felix and Festus

The Jerusalem church hosts a conference in A.D. 49

Nero's addition to Agrippa's realm

MEDITERRANEAN SEA

PHOENICIA
Sidon
Tyre
Ptolemais (Acco)
Dora
Caesarea Maritima
Apollonia
Joppa

Chalcis
Abila
Da

Mt. Hermon
Caesarea-Philippi
L. Huleh

GAULANITIS
Naveh
BATANEA
Rap

Gischala (Gush Halav)
Capernaum Bethsaida
GALILEE
Sepphoris Taricheae Sea of Galilee Gamala
Nazareth Tiberias Hippos
Mt. Carmel
Mt. Tabor Gadara
Abila
Yarmuk R.

Litani R.
Kishon R.
Mt. Gilboa Scythopolis (Beth-shan)
Pella Dion
DECAPOLIS

SAMARIA
Sebaste (Samaria)
Mt. Ebal Neapolis (Shechem)
Antipatris (Aphek) Mt. Gerizim
Yarkon R.
W. Farah
Jordan R.
Jabbok R.
Gerasa (Jerash)

Lydda
JUDEA
Jamnia Emmaus (Nicopolis)
Azotus (Ashdod)
Ascalon (Ashkelon)
Eleutheropolis (Beth-guvrin)
Gaza

Jericho
Jerusalem
Judean Wilderness
En-gedi
DEAD SEA

PEREA
Gedor (Gadara)
Philadelphia (Amma

Esbus (Heshbon)
Abila Livias Medeba
Julius Mt. Nebo

Machaerus
Callirrhoe

IDUMEA
Arad Masada
Beersheba

NABATEA
Arabah
N. Besor
Zered R.

0   10
0   10   20

90 ▶ PENTECOST AND THE JEWISH DIASPORA

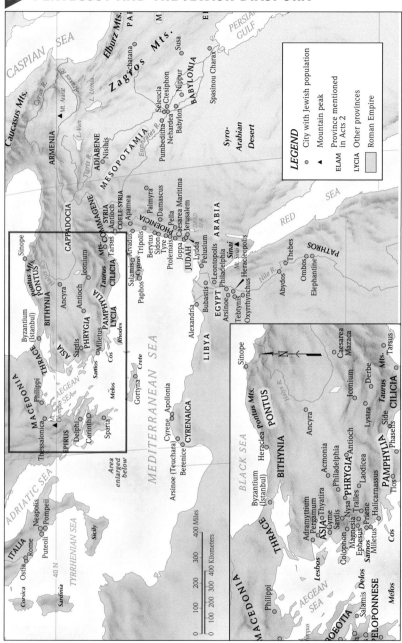

Acts 2:8-11

How is it that we hear, each of us, in our own native language? Parthians, Medes, Elamites; those who live in Mesopotamia, in Judea and Cappadocia, Pontus and Asia, Phrygia and Pamphylia, Egypt and the parts of Libya near Cyrene; visitors from Rome, both Jews and proselytes, Cretans and Arabs—we hear them speaking in our own languages the magnificent acts of God."

91 EXPANSION OF THE EARLY CHURCH IN PALESTINE

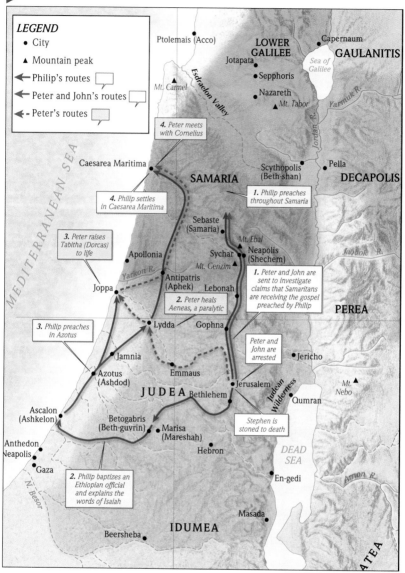

LEGEND
- • City
- ▲ Mountain peak
- ← Philip's routes
- ← Peter and John's routes
- ←- Peter's routes

4. Peter meets with Cornelius

4. Philip settles in Caesarea Maritima

3. Peter raises Tabitha (Dorcas) to life

1. Philip preaches throughout Samaria

1. Peter and John are sent to investigate claims that Samaritans are receiving the gospel preached by Philip

2. Peter heals Aeneas, a paralytic

3. Philip preaches in Azotus

Peter and John are arrested

Stephen is stoned to death

2. Philip baptizes an Ethiopian official and explains the words of Isaiah

Ptolemais (Acco), LOWER GALILEE, GAULANITIS, Capernaum, Sea of Galilee, Jotapata, Sepphoris, Nazareth, Mt. Carmel, Mt. Tabor, Esdraelon Valley, Jordan R., Yarmuk R., Caesarea Maritima, SAMARIA, Scythopolis (Beth-shan), Pella, DECAPOLIS, Sebaste (Samaria), Mt. Ebal, Neapolis (Shechem), Sychar, Mt. Gerizim, Jabbok R., Apollonia, Yarkon R., Antipatris (Aphek), Lebonah, Joppa, Lydda, Gophna, PEREA, Jamnia, Emmaus, Jericho, Mt. Nebo, Azotus (Ashdod), JUDEA, Bethlehem, Jerusalem, Judean Wilderness, Qumran, Ascalon (Ashkelon), Betogabris (Beth-guvrin), Marisa (Mareshah), Hebron, DEAD SEA, En-gedi, Anthedon Neapolis, Gaza, N. Besor, Amon R., Masada, Beersheba, IDUMEA, MEDITERRANEAN SEA

Acts 8:1-5

Saul agreed with putting him to death.

On that day a severe persecution broke out against the church in Jerusalem, and all except the apostles were scattered throughout the land of Judea and Samaria. But devout men buried Stephen and mourned deeply over him. Saul, however, was ravaging the church, and he would enter house after house, drag off men and women, and put them in prison.

So those who were scattered went on their way proclaiming the message of good news. Philip went down to a city in Samaria and preached the Messiah to them.

92 PAUL'S CONVERSION AND EARLY MINISTRY

COMMAGENE

Taurus Mountains

Cilician Gates

CILICIA

Tarsus

Issus

Syrian Gates

Amanus Mts.

Antioch

6. Paul and Barnabas establish a strong church where believers were first called Christians

Seleucia Pieria

Aleppo

Euphrates R.

LEGEND
- • City
- ▲ Mountain peak
- ⊃⊂ Pass
- ← Paul sent to Damascus
- ◄··· Paul spends time in Arabia
- ← Paul returns to Jerusalem
- ← Paul flees from Hellenists
- ← Paul and Barnabas travel to Antioch
- ← Paul and Barnabas sent to Jerusalem
- ← Paul and Barnabas return to Antioch
- ☐ Kingdom of Agrippa I

7. Paul and Barnabas travel to Jerusalem with aid for famine

SYRIA

Hamath

Emesa

8. Paul and Barnabas return to Antioch

Palmyra (Tadmor)

Orontes R.

Tripolis

Byblos

Litani R.

COELE-SYRIA

3. Paul baptized and preaches about his newfound faith

Sidon

Mt. Hermon

Damascus

2. Paul has a vision of Jesus and converts

5. Paul returns to his hometown of Tarsus

Tyre

PHOENICIA

Caesarea-Philippi

Capernaum

Canatha (Kenath)

Ptolemais (Acco)

Tiberias

Gamala

▲ Mt. Hauran

Caesarea Maritima

Scythopolis

Bostra

MEDITERRANEAN SEA

Antipatris

Pella

Joppa

4. Paul flees to Arabia then returns to Jerusalem

Azotus (Ashdod)

JUDEA

Jabbok R.

Philadelphia (Amman)

Gaza

Jerusalem

Jericho

Raphia

IDUMEA

DEAD SEA

Syro-Arabian Desert

1. Paul sanctioned to arrest followers in Damascus

N

Arabah

NABATEA

0 25 50 75 100 Miles

0 25 50 75 100 Kilometers

Galatians 1:18-21

Then after three years I did go up to Jerusalem to get to know Cephas, and I stayed with him 15 days.

But I didn't see any of the other apostles except James, the Lord's brother. Now in what I write to you, I'm not lying. God is my witness.

Afterwards, I went to the regions of Syria and Cilicia.

93 THE FIRST MISSIONARY JOURNEY OF PAUL

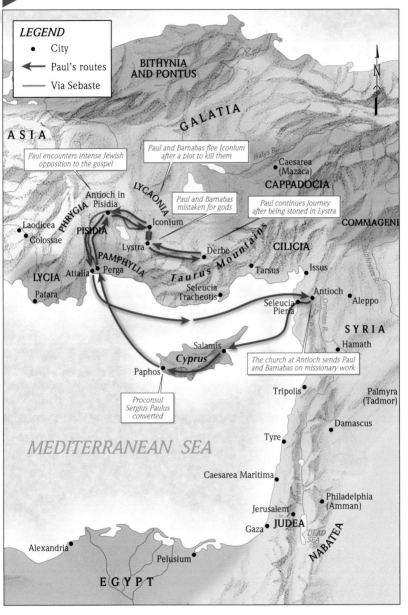

LEGEND
- City
← Paul's routes
— Via Sebaste

Paul encounters intense Jewish opposition to the gospel

Paul and Barnabas flee Iconium after a plot to kill them

Paul and Barnabas mistaken for gods

Paul continues journey after being stoned in Lystra

The church at Antioch sends Paul and Barnabas on missionary work

Proconsul Sergius Paulus converted

BITHYNIA AND PONTUS

GALATIA

ASIA

Halys R.

Caesarea (Mazaca)

CAPPADOCIA

COMMAGENE

LYCAONIA

Antioch in Pisidia

PHRYGIA

PISIDIA

Laodicea

Colossae

Iconium

Lystra

Derbe

CILICIA

Tarsus

Issus

Taurus Mountains

Euphrates R.

PAMPHYLIA

LYCIA

Attalia

Perga

Patara

Seleucia Tracheotis

Antioch

Aleppo

Seleucia Pieria

Orontes R.

SYRIA

Salamis

Cyprus

Hamath

Paphos

Tripolis

Palmyra (Tadmor)

Damascus

MEDITERRANEAN SEA

Tyre

Caesarea Maritima

Jordan R.

Philadelphia (Amman)

Jerusalem

Gaza

JUDEA

DEAD SEA

NABATEA

Alexandria

Pelusium

EGYPT

N

Acts 13:4-5

Being sent out by the Holy Spirit, they came down to Seleucia, and from there they sailed to Cyprus.

Arriving in Salamis, they proclaimed God's message in the Jewish synagogues. They also had John as their assistant.

94▶ THE SECOND MISSIONARY JOURNEY OF PAUL

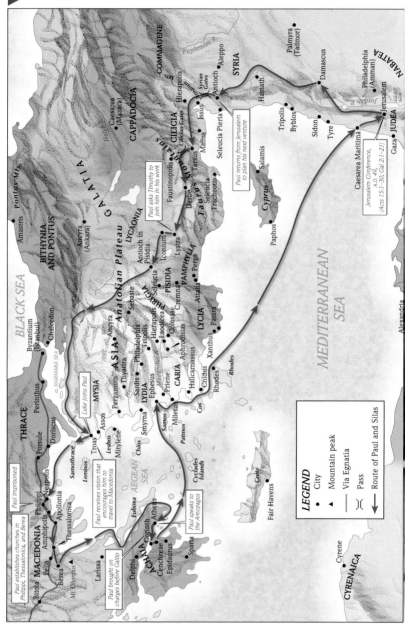

Acts 16:6-9

They went through the region of Phrygia and Galatia and were prevented by the Holy Spirit from speaking the message in the province of Asia. When they came to Mysia, they tried to go into Bithynia, but the Spirit of Jesus did not allow them. So, bypassing Mysia, they came down to Troas. During the night a vision appeared to Paul: a Macedonian man was standing and pleading with him, "Cross over to Macedonia and help us!"

95 THE THIRD MISSIONARY JOURNEY OF PAUL

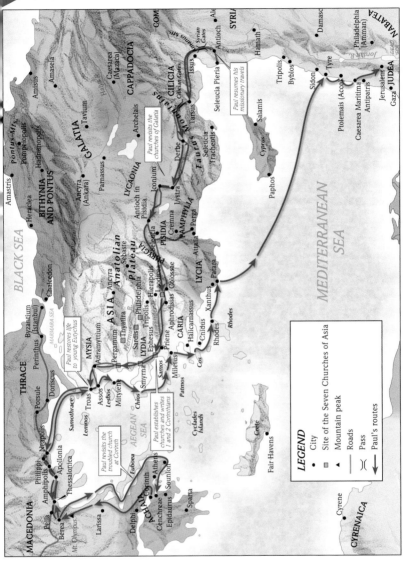

Acts 20:13-17

Then we went on ahead to the ship and sailed for Assos, from there intending to take Paul on board. For these were his instructions, since he himself was going by land. When he met us at Assos, we took him on board and came to Mitylene. Sailing from there, the next day we arrived off Chios. The following day we crossed over to Samos, and the day after, we came to Miletus. For Paul had decided to sail past Ephesus so he would not have to spend time in the province of Asia, because he was hurrying to be in Jerusalem, if possible, for the day of Pentecost.

Now from Miletus, he sent to Ephesus and called for the elders of the church.

96 ▶ PAUL'S ARREST AND IMPRISONMENT

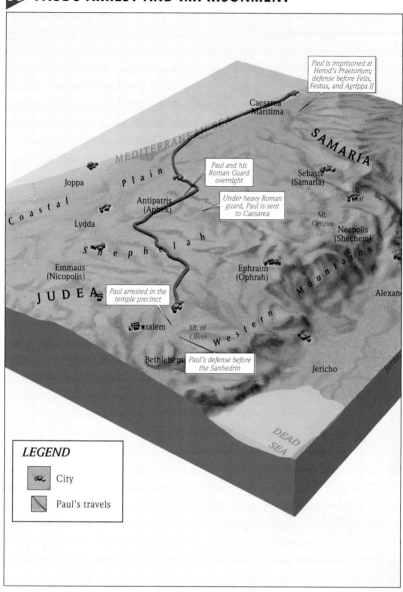

Paul is imprisoned at Herod's Praetorium; defense before Felix, Festus, and Agrippa II

Caesarea Maritima

SAMARIA

Joppa

plain

Sebaste (Samaria)

Mt. Ebal

Paul and his Roman Guard overnight

Antipatris (Aphek)

Under heavy Roman guard, Paul is sent to Caesarea

Mt. Gerizim

Neapolis (Shechem)

Coastal

Lydda

Shephelah

Emmaus (Nicopolis)

Ephraim (Ophrah)

Mountains

Alexan

JUDEA

Paul arrested in the temple precinct

Jerusalem

Mt. of Olives

Western

Bethlehem

Paul's defense before the Sanhedrin

Jericho

DEAD SEA

LEGEND

City

Paul's travels

Acts 23:31-33

Therefore, during the night, the soldiers took Paul and brought him to Antipatris as they were ordered. The next day, they returned to the barracks, allowing the cavalry to go on with him. When these men entered Caesarea and delivered the letter to the governor, they also presented Paul to him.

97▶ PAUL'S VOYAGE TO ROME

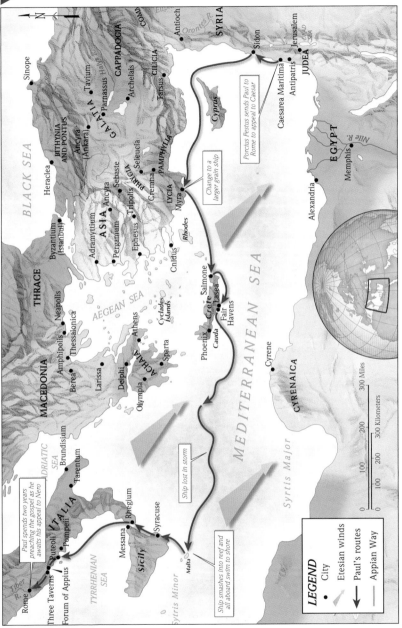

Acts 27:4-7

When we had put out to sea from there, we sailed along the northern coast of Cyprus because the winds were against us. After sailing through the open sea off Cilicia and Pamphylia, we reached Myra in Lycia. There the centurion found an Alexandrian ship sailing for Italy and put us on board. Sailing slowly for many days, we came with difficulty as far as Cnidus. But since the wind did not allow us to approach it, we sailed along the south side of Crete off Salmone.

98 THE FIRST JEWISH REVOLT

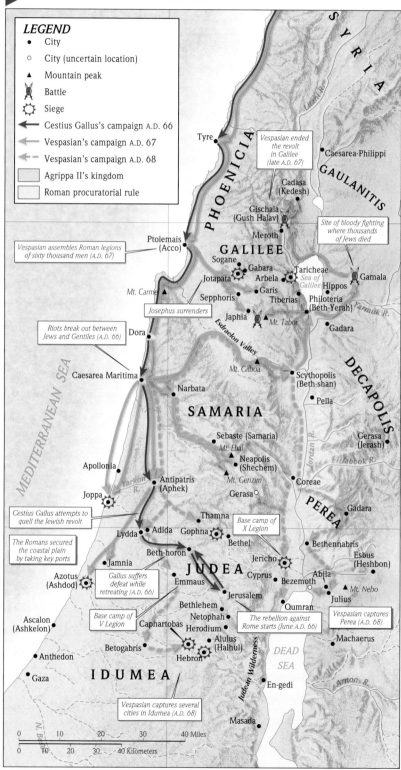

LEGEND
- • City
- ○ City (uncertain location)
- ▲ Mountain peak
- Battle
- Siege
- ← Cestius Gallus's campaign A.D. 66
- ← Vespasian's campaign A.D. 67
- ←-- Vespasian's campaign A.D. 68
- Agrippa II's kingdom
- Roman procuratorial rule

Vespasian ended the revolt in Galilee (late A.D. 67)

Site of bloody fighting where thousands of Jews died

Vespasian assembles Roman legions of sixty thousand men (A.D. 67)

Josephus surrenders

Riots break out between Jews and Gentiles (A.D. 66)

Cestius Gallus attempts to quell the Jewish revolt

The Romans secured the coastal plain by taking key ports

Gallus suffers defeat while retreating (A.D. 66)

Base camp of X Legion

Base camp of V Legion

The rebellion against Rome starts (June A.D. 66)

Vespasian captures Perea (A.D. 68)

Vespasian captures several cities in Idumea (A.D. 68)

SYRIA

PHOENICIA

GAULANITIS

GALILEE

DECAPOLIS

SAMARIA

PEREA

JUDEA

IDUMEA

MEDITERRANEAN SEA

DEAD SEA

Tyre
Caesarea-Philippi
Cadasa (Kedesh)
Gischala (Gush Halav)
Meroth
Ptolemais (Acco)
Sogane
Gabara
Taricheae
Gamala
Jotapata
Arbela
Hippos
Sepphoris
Garis
Philoteria (Beth-Yerah)
Mt. Carmel
Tiberias
Japhia
Mt. Tabor
Gadara
Dora
Esdraelon Valley
Mt. Gilboa
Scythopolis (Beth-shan)
Caesarea Maritima
Narbata
Pella
Sebaste (Samaria)
Mt. Ebal
Gerasa (Jerash)
Apollonia
Neapolis (Shechem)
Antipatris (Aphek)
Mt. Gerizim
Joppa
Gerasa
Coreae
Gadara
Thamna
Lydda
Adida
Gophna
Bethel
Bethennabris
Beth-horon
Jericho
Esbus (Heshbon)
Jamnia
Cyprus
Abila
Azotus (Ashdod)
Emmaus
Bezemoth
Mt. Nebo
Jerusalem
Julius
Ascalon (Ashkelon)
Bethlehem
Qumran
Caphartobas
Netophah
Herodium
Machaerus
Betogabris
Alulus (Halhul)
Hebron
En-gedi
Anthedon
Gaza
Masada
Sea of Galilee
Yarmuk R.
Jordan R.
Jabbok R.
Yarkon R.
Litani R.
Arnon R.
N. Besor
Judean Wilderness

0   10   20   30   40 Miles
0 10 20 30 40 Kilometers

99▶ TITUS'S CAMPAIGNS/THE SIEGE OF JERUSALEM

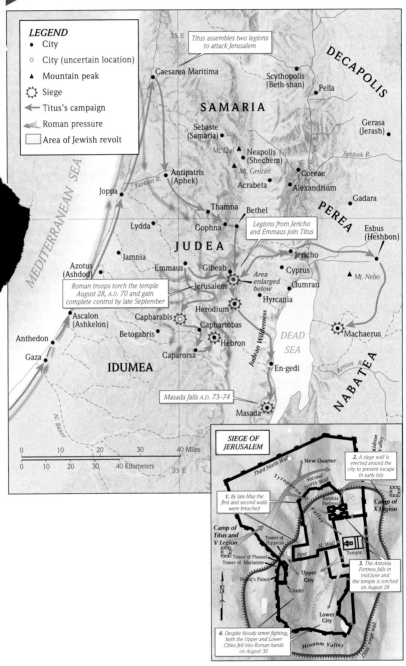

LEGEND
- • City
- ○ City (uncertain location)
- ▲ Mountain peak
- ✺ Siege
- ◀ Titus's campaign
- ◀ Roman pressure
- ☐ Area of Jewish revolt

Titus assembles two legions to attack Jerusalem

35 E

DECAPOLIS

Caesarea Maritima
Scythopolis (Beth-shan)
Pella

SAMARIA

Sebaste (Samaria)
Gerasa (Jerash)

Mt. Ebal ▲
Neapolis (Shechem)
▲ Mt. Gerizim
Jabbok R.

Antipatris (Aphek)
Coreae

Joppa
Yarkon R.
Acrabeta
Alexandrium

Gadara

Thamna
Bethel

PEREA

Lydda
Gophna
Legions from Jericho and Emmaus join Titus

Esbus (Heshbon)

JUDEA

Jamnia
Emmaus
Gibeah
Jericho
Cyprus

▲ Mt. Nebo

Azotus (Ashdod)
Area enlarged below
Qumran

Roman troops torch the temple August 28, A.D. 70 and gain complete control by late September

Jerusalem
Hyrcania

Herodium

MEDITERRANEAN SEA

Ascalon (Ashkelon)
Capharabis
Caphartobas
Machaerus

Anthedon
Betogabris
Hebron

Gaza
Caparorsa
En-gedi

IDUMEA

DEAD SEA

Judean Wilderness

Arnon R.

NABATEA

Masada falls A.D. 73–74
Masada

0 10 20 30 40 Miles
0 10 20 30 40 Kilometers
35 E
N. Besor

SIEGE OF JERUSALEM

Kidron Valley

Third North Wall
New Quarter

2. A siege wall is erected around the city to prevent escape in early July

Tyropoeon
Second North Wall

1. By late May the first and second walls were breached

Antonia Fortress
Camp of X Legion

Camp of Titus and V Legion

Tower of Hippicus
Tower of Phasael
Tower of Marianne
First
N. Wall
Temple

3. The Antonia Fortress falls in mid-June and the temple is torched on August 28

Herod's Palace
Upper City

Citadel

Lower City

4. Despite bloody street fighting, both the Upper and Lower Cities fell into Roman hands on August 30

Hinnom Valley

Titus siege wall

100 REVELATION 2–3

John writes Revelation encouraging Christians to remain faithful.

LEGEND
- City
- Cities of the Seven Churches
- Major road

Revelation 1:19-20

Therefore write what you have seen, what is, and what will take place after this. The secret of the seven stars you saw in My right hand, and of the seven gold lampstands, is this: the seven stars are the angels of the seven churches, and the seven lampstands are the seven churches.

101 THE EXPANSION OF CHRISTIANITY IN THE SECOND AND THIRD CENTURIES A.D.

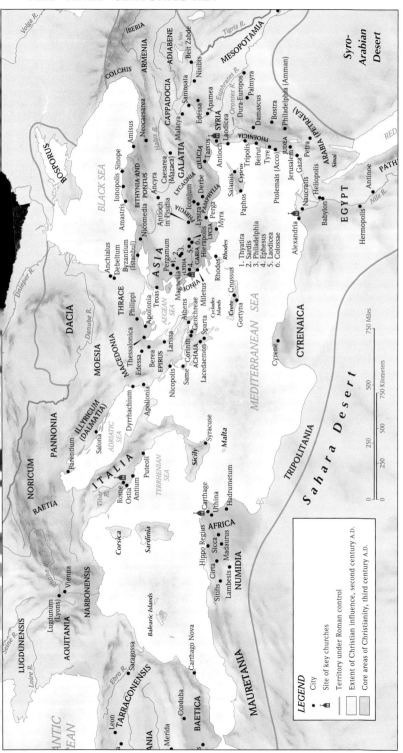

LEGEND
- City
- Site of key churches
- Territory under Roman control
- Extent of Christian influence, second century A.D.
- Core areas of Christianity, third century A.D.

1. Thyatira
2. Sardis
3. Philadelphia
4. Ephesus
5. Laodicea
6. Colossae

PHOTO AND ART CREDITS
(All Rights Reserved)

Arnold, Nancy
19, 30, 43

Biblical Illustrator – Ernie Couch
22

Biblical Illustrator – David Rogers
7, 25, 41, 60

Biblical Illustrator – Bob Schatz
22, 51

Biblical Illustrator – Ken Touchton
23, 26, 29, 31, 32, 33, 69

Brisco, Thomas V.
12, 14, 36, 42, 43, 46, 50

Langston, Scott
25, 28, 31, 45, 56, 57

Scofield Collection, Dargan Research Library, Nashville, Tennessee
7, 22, 27, 40, 65, 71

Stephens, William H.
48

Tolar, William B.
40, 54